BAKE ME A CAKE

COLLINS & BROWN

The Good Housekeeping website is
www.goodhousekeeping.co.uk

ISBN 978-1-908449-92-4

A catalogue record for this book is available from
the British Library.

Reproduction by Dot Gradations Ltd, UK
Printed and bound by
1010 Printing International Ltd, China

This book can be ordered direct from the publisher.
Contact the marketing department, but try your
bookshop first.

www.anovabooks.com

NOTES

Both metric and imperial measures are given for
the recipes. Follow either set of measures, not a
mixture of both, as they are not interchangeable.

All spoon measures are level.
1 tsp = 5ml spoon; 1 tbsp = 15ml spoon.

Ovens and grills must be preheated to the specified
temperature.

Medium eggs should be used except where
otherwise specified. Free-range eggs are
recommended.

Note that some recipes contain raw or lightly
cooked eggs. The young, elderly, pregnant women
and anyone with an immune-deficiency disease
should avoid these because of the slight risk
of salmonella.

Contents

Classic Cakes

The Golden Rules

Cake recipes vary greatly, not only by the methods used to make the cakes, but also in the balance of the various ingredients. There are no secrets to making a great cake – all you need to do is follow these simple golden rules.

If making larger cakes, check first that your oven is big enough. There should be at least 5cm (2in) oven space all around the cake tin to ensure that it cooks evenly.

Always make sure you have the correct tin shape and size according to the recipe you are making. The tin sizes quoted in this book refer to the base measurement of the tin.

Ensure the tin is properly prepared and lined for baking the recipe you have chosen to make.

Check that you have all the necessary ingredients stated in the recipe and that they are at the right temperature.

Weigh out and/or measure all the ingredients accurately using scales, measuring spoons and a measuring jug. Always work in either metric or imperial.

Use the egg sizes stated in the recipe. Substituting different sizes can affect the balance of the cake mixture.

Sifting dry ingredients together helps not only to aerate, but also to disperse lumps.

Store flours and raising agents in well-sealed packets or airtight containers in a cool, dry place.

When making cakes by hand, beat well with a wooden spoon until the mixture is light and fluffy (only possible if your butter is at the correct temperature).

Be careful not to over-process or over-beat the mixture; the mixture can over-rise in the oven, then collapse and dip in the centre during baking.

Always scrape down the mixture with a spatula during mixing (remember to turn off any electric mixers first).

If ingredients have to be folded into a cake mixture, use a large metal spoon, which will cut cleanly through the mixture. Keep scooping down to the bottom of the bowl, then turning the mixture on top of itself, while at the same time giving the bowl a quarter twist. Continue just until the ingredients are combined – do not be tempted to over-fold the cake mixture. Try not to be heavy-handed when folding in flour.

Don't let a cake mixture sit around once you've made it: pop it straight into the cake tin and into the oven, otherwise the raising agents will start to react.

Before any baking, check the temperature of your oven is correct by investing in an inexpensive oven thermometer. Check your oven is preheated to the correct temperature stated in the recipe.

Once the cake is in the oven, resist the temptation to open the oven door before at least three-quarters of the specified baking time has passed – the heat will escape and the cake will sink.

If your cake appears to be browning too quickly, cover the top loosely with foil or greaseproof paper towards the end of cooking.

If conditions are cold, the mixture will take longer to cook. Similarly, if it is a very hot day, then baking will be slightly quicker.

Always check the cake is cooked 5–10 minutes before the given baking time, just in case the oven is a little fast.

After it has come out of the oven, leave the cake to cool in the tin for the specified time and then turn out on to a wire rack to cool completely.

Let the tins cool completely before washing them in warm, soapy water with a non-abrasive sponge.

Basic Baking Equipment

A selection of basic equipment is compulsory in order to bake and decorate cakes successfully. Start with a few basic items and add to your collection as your skills increase (and as the demands of the recipe dictate).

Scales

Accurate measurement is essential when following most baking recipes. The electronic scale is the most accurate and can weigh up to 2kg (4½lb) or 5kg (11lb) in increments of 1–5g. Buy one with a flat platform on which you can put your bowl or measuring jug. Always set the scale to zero before adding the ingredients.

Measuring jugs, cups and spoons

Jugs can be plastic or glass, and are available, marked with both metric and imperial, in sizes ranging from 500ml (17fl oz) to 2 litres (3½ pints), or even 3 litres (5¼ pints). Measuring cups are bought in sets of ¼, ⅓, ½ and 1 cups. A standard 1 cup measure is equivalent to about 250ml (9fl oz). Measuring spoons are useful for the smallest units and accurate spoon measurements go up to 15ml (1 tbsp).

These may be in plastic or metal and often come in sets attached together on a ring.

Mixing bowls

Stainless steel bowls work best when you are using a hand-held whisk, or when you need to place the bowl into a larger bowl filled with iced water for chilling down or to place it over simmering water (when melting chocolate, for example). Plastic or glass bowls are best if you need to use them in the microwave. Bowls with gently tapered sides – much wider at the rim than at the base – will be useful for mixing dough.

Mixing spoons

For general mixing, the cheap and sturdy wooden spoon still can't be beaten. The spoon should be stiff, so that it can cope with thick mixtures such as dough. In addition, a large metal spoon for folding ingredients together is an invaluable item to have.

Bakeware

As well as being thin enough to conduct heat quickly and efficiently, bakeware should be sturdy enough not to warp. Most bakeware is made from aluminium, and it may have enamel or non-stick coatings. A newer material for some bakeware is flexible, oven-safe silicone.

It is safe to touch straight from the oven, is inherently non-stick and is also flexible – making it a lot easier to remove muffins and other bakes from their pans than it used to be.

Baking trays/Baking sheets

Shallower than a roasting tin, these have many uses in baking. To avoid having to bake in batches, choose ones that are large (but which fit comfortably in your oven). Buy the best you can afford.

Baking dishes

Are usually ceramic or Pyrex and you should have them in several sizes, ranging from 15-23cm (6-9in) to 25.5-35.5cm (10-14in).

Cake tins

Available in many shapes and sizes, tins may be single-piece, loose-based or springform.

Loaf tins

Available in various sizes, but one of the most useful is a 900g (2lb) tin.

Pie tins

You should have both single-piece tins and loose-based tins for flans and pies.

Muffin tins

These come in various sizes and depths and are available in both aluminium and silicone. If you make a lot of muffins and cupcakes it's worth investing in different types.

Victoria Sandwich

Hands-on time: 20 minutes
Cooking time: about 25 minutes, plus cooling

175g (6oz) unsalted butter, softened, plus extra to grease

175g (6oz) caster sugar

3 medium eggs

175g (6oz) self-raising flour, sifted

3-4 tbsp jam (strawberry or raspberry is most traditional)

icing or caster sugar

1 Preheat the oven to 190°C (170°C fan oven) mark 5. Grease two 18cm (7in) sandwich tins and base-line with greaseproof paper.

2 Put the butter and caster sugar into a large bowl and, using a hand-held electric whisk, beat together until pale and fluffy. Add the eggs one at a time, beating well after each addition – add a spoonful of the flour if the mixture looks as if it's about to curdle.

3 Once the eggs are added, use a large metal spoon to fold in the remaining flour. Divide the mixture evenly between the prepared tins and level the surface.

4 Bake both cakes on the middle shelf of the oven for 20-25 minutes until well risen and springy to the touch when lightly pressed in the centre. Loosen the edges with a palette knife and leave to cool in the tins for 10 minutes.

5 Turn out and peel off the lining paper, then transfer to a wire rack and leave to cool completely.

6 Sandwich the two cakes together with jam and dust with icing sugar, or sprinkle the top with caster sugar. Serve in slices.

Cuts into 10 slices

Chocolate Victoria Sandwich

Hands-on time: 20 minutes
Cooking time: 20 minutes, plus cooling

175g (6oz) unsalted butter at room
   temperature, plus extra to grease

3 tbsp cocoa powder

175g (6oz) golden caster sugar

3 medium eggs, beaten

160g (5½oz) self-raising flour, sifted

golden caster sugar to dredge

For the filling

1 tbsp cocoa powder

75g (3oz) unsalted butter, softened

175g (6oz) icing sugar, sifted

a few drops of vanilla extract

1–2 tbsp milk or water

1 Preheat the oven to 190°C (170°C fan
   oven) mark 5. Grease two 18cm (7in)
   sandwich tins and base-line with
   baking parchment. Blend the cocoa
   powder with 3 tbsp hot water to make
   a smooth paste, then leave to cool.

2 Put the butter and sugar into a large
   bowl and, using a freestanding mixer
   or hand-held electric whisk, cream
   together until pale and fluffy. Add the
   cooled cocoa mixture and beat until
   evenly blended.

3 Add the beaten eggs, a little at a time,
   beating well after each addition. Using
   a metal spoon or large spatula, fold
   in half the flour, then carefully fold in
   the rest. Divide the mixture evenly
   between the prepared tins and level
   the surface.

4 Bake both cakes on the middle shelf
   of the oven for about 20 minutes
   until well risen, springy to the touch
   when lightly pressed and beginning
   to shrink away from the sides of the
   tins. Loosen the edges with a palette
   knife and leave to cool in the tins for
   5 minutes, then turn out on to a wire
   rack, peel off the lining paper and
   leave to cool completely.

5 To make the chocolate buttercream
   filling, blend the cocoa powder with
   3 tbsp boiling water and leave to cool.
   Put the butter into a bowl and beat
   with a wooden spoon until light and
   fluffy. Gradually stir in the icing sugar.

Add the blended cocoa, vanilla extract and milk or water and beat well until light and smooth.

6 Sandwich the two cakes together with the chocolate buttercream and sprinkle the top with caster sugar. Serve in slices.

SAVE TIME

Store in an airtight container in a cool place. It will keep for up to one week.

Cuts into 10 slices

15

Whisked Sponge

Hands-on time: 25 minutes
Cooking time: about 25 minutes, plus cooling

unsalted butter to grease

90g (3¼oz) plain flour, plus extra to dust

3 large eggs

125g (4oz) caster sugar

For the filling and topping

3–4 tbsp strawberry, raspberry or
   apricot jam

125ml (4fl oz) whipping or double cream,
   whipped (optional)

icing or caster sugar

1 Preheat the oven to 190°C (170°C fan oven) mark 5. Grease and base-line two 18cm (7in) sandwich tins, grease the paper lightly and dust the sides with a little flour.

2 Put the eggs and caster sugar into a large heatproof bowl and, using a hand-held electric whisk, beat until well blended. Put the bowl over a pan of hot water, making sure the base of the bowl doesn't touch the water, and whisk until the mixture is pale and creamy and thick enough to leave a trail on the surface when the whisk is lifted – this should take about 5 minutes. Remove the bowl from the pan and carry on whisking until cool.

3 Sift half the flour into the mixture and, using a large metal spoon or spatula, fold it in very lightly (trying to knock out as little air as possible). Sift in the remaining flour and repeat the folding process until combined.

4 Divide the mixture evenly between the prepared tins, tilting the tins to spread the mixture evenly (do not bang on the worksurface as this will knock out valuable air).

5 Bake both cakes on the middle shelf of the oven for 20–25 minutes until well risen and springy to the touch when lightly pressed in the centre (do not test with a skewer, as this can cause the cake to sink). Loosen the edges with a palette knife and turn the cakes out on to a wire rack to cool.

6 When the cakes are cold, peel off the lining paper and sandwich the cakes

together with jam and whipped cream, if you like. Dust with icing sugar, or sprinkle the top with caster sugar.

This classic fatless sponge does not keep well and is best eaten on the day it is made. Serve in slices.

Cuts into 6–8 slices

Take 5 Basic Cake Ingredients

Fat

Unsalted butter gives the best results in most recipes. Margarine can be substituted in many recipes, although it doesn't lend such a good flavour, but low-fat 'spreads', with their high water content, are not suitable. For most cake recipes, you need to use the fat at room temperature. If necessary, you can soften it, cautiously, in the microwave.

Eggs

Eggs should also be used at room temperature; if taken straight from the fridge they are more likely to curdle a cake mixture. Make sure you use the correct size – unless otherwise stated, medium eggs should be used in all the recipes. A fresh egg should feel heavy in your hand and will sink to the bottom of the bowl or float on its side when put into water. Older eggs, over two weeks old, will float vertically.

Sugar

Golden caster sugar is generally used for cakes, but for a richer colour and flavour, light or dark muscovado sugars can be substituted. Icing sugar is ideal for icings, frostings and buttercreams.

Flour

Self-raising white flour is used in most cake recipes, as it provides a raising agent, whereas plain white flour is generally used for biscuits and cookies. Plain or self-raising wholemeal flour can be substituted, although the results will be darker and denser and nuttier in flavour. Half white and half wholemeal makes a good compromise if you want to incorporate extra fibre. If you sift it before use, tip the bran left in the sieve into the bowl.

Nuts

Some nuts can be bought ready-prepared, others need preparation. After nuts have been shelled, they are still coated with a skin, which, although edible, tastes bitter. This is easier to remove if the nuts are blanched or toasted. To blanch, put the shelled nuts into a bowl and cover with boiling water. Leave for 2 minutes, then drain. Remove the skins by rubbing the nuts in a teatowel or squeezing between your thumb and index finger.

Toasting also improves the flavour. Preheat the oven to 200°C (180°C fan oven) mark 6. Put the shelled nuts on a baking sheet in a single layer and bake for 8–15 minutes until the skins are lightly coloured. Remove the skins by rubbing the nuts in a teatowel.

Unless you want very large pieces, the easiest way to chop nuts is to put the cold, skinned nuts in a food processor and pulse at 10-second intervals. Or, place a chopping

board on a folded teatowel on the worksurface and use a cook's knife to chop to the size of coarse breadcrumbs. Only chop about 75g (3oz) of nuts at a time. Store in an airtight container for up to two weeks.

To slice nuts, put them on a board and, using a cook's knife, carefully slice the nuts as thinly as required. To make slivers, carefully cut the slices to make narrow matchsticks.

Genoese Sponge

40g (1½oz) unsalted butter, plus extra
  to grease

65g (2½oz) plain flour, plus extra to dust

3 large eggs

75g (3oz) caster sugar

1 tbsp cornflour

For the filling and topping

3-4 tbsp strawberry, raspberry or
  apricot jam

125ml (4fl oz) whipping cream, whipped
  (optional)

icing sugar or caster sugar

1 Grease two 18cm (7in) sandwich tins
  or one deep 18cm (7in) round cake tin,
  base-line with greaseproof paper
  and dust the sides with a little flour.

2 Put the butter into a small pan and
  heat gently to melt, then take off
  the heat and leave to stand for a few
  minutes to cool slightly.

3 Put the eggs and sugar into a bowl
  and, using a hand-held electric whisk,
  beat until well blended. Place the bowl
  over a pan of hot water, making sure
  the base of the bowl doesn't touch the
  water, and whisk until the mixture is
  pale and creamy and thick enough to
  leave a trail on the surface when the
  whisk is lifted – this should take about
  5 minutes. Remove the bowl from the
  pan and whisk until cool.

4 Preheat the oven to 180°C (160°C fan
  oven) mark 4. Sift the plain flour
  and cornflour into the egg bowl,
  then use a large metal spoon to
  carefully fold in (trying to knock
  out as little air as possible).

5 Pour the melted and cooled butter
  around the edges of the mixture,
  leaving any butter sediment behind in
  the pan. Very lightly, fold in the butter
  until it has been incorporated into the
  mixture. Pour into the prepared tin(s).

6 Bake the cake(s) on the middle shelf
  of the oven for 25–30 minutes for
  the sandwich tins, or 35–40 minutes
  for the deep tin, until well risen and
  springy to the touch when lightly

pressed in the centre. Loosen the edges with a palette knife and leave to cool in the tin(s) for 10 minutes. Turn out on to a wire rack (leave the lining paper on) and leave to cool completely.

7 When the cake(s) is cold, peel off the lining paper (and halve the single cake horizontally) and sandwich the two cakes/halves together with jam and whipped cream, if you like. Dust with icing sugar, or sprinkle the top with caster sugar. Serve in slices.

Cuts into 6 large slices

Madeira Cake

Hands-on time: 20 minutes
Cooking time: about 1¾ minutes, plus cooling

275g (10oz) unsalted butter, softened, plus extra to grease

175g (6oz) plain flour

175g (6oz) self-raising flour

275g (10oz) caster sugar

5 medium eggs, lightly beaten

lemon juice or milk

1 Preheat the oven to 170°C (150°C fan oven) mark 3. Grease and line a deep 20.5cm (8in) round cake tin, then grease the paper lightly.

2 Sift the flours together. Cream the butter and sugar together in a separate bowl until pale and fluffy. Gradually add the eggs, beating well after each addition.

3 Using a large metal spoon, fold the flours into the butter mixture, adding a little lemon juice or milk if necessary to give a dropping consistency.

4 Turn the mixture into the prepared tin and level the surface. Using the back of a metal spoon, make a slight depression in the middle of the surface of the cake to ensure that it doesn't mound/dome too much while baking.

5 Bake on the middle shelf of the oven for about 1½–1¾ hours until the cake springs back when lightly pressed in the centre. Leave to cool in the tin for 15 minutes, then turn out on to a wire rack and leave to cool completely.

6 When the cake is cold, wrap in clingfilm or foil and store in a cool place until required. Serve in slices.

SAVE TIME

Store in an airtight container. It will keep for up to one week or can be frozen for up to one month.

Cuts into 12 slices

Chocolate Ganache Recipe

Ever popular, this ganache icing is ideal for covering cakes for an elegant finish. Use ganache at room temperature as a smooth coating for cakes, or chill it lightly until thickened and use to fill meringues, choux buns or sandwich cakes. This ganache is not hugely sweet, so if you are making it for children add 1 tbsp golden syrup to the chocolate bowl in step 1.

Basic Mixture

To make 225g (8oz), enough to cover an 18cm (7in) round cake, you will need:

225g (8oz) plain chocolate, (with 60-70% cocoa solids), roughly chopped and 250ml (9fl oz) double cream.

1. Put the chocolate into a medium heatproof bowl. Pour the cream into a pan and bring to the boil.
2. As soon as the cream comes to the boil, pour it into the chocolate bowl and stir gently until the chocolate has melted and the mixture is smooth. Put to one side for 5 minutes.
3. Whisk the ganache until it begins to hold its shape. Used at room temperature, the mixture should be the consistency of softened butter.

Take 5 Variations

Coffee
Stir in 1 tsp instant coffee (liquid or granules) or a shot of espresso when melting the chocolate.

Spiced
Add a pinch of ground cinnamon, crushed cardamom seeds, a pinch of cayenne pepper or freshly grated nutmeg to the melting chocolate.

Vanilla
Stir in ¼ tsp vanilla extract when melting the chocolate.

Rum, Whisky or Cognac
Stir in about 1 tsp alcohol when melting the chocolate.

Butter
Stir in 25g (1oz) butter towards the end of heating the milk.

Marble Cake

🍴 **Hands-on time:** 25 minutes
Cooking time: about 1 hour, plus cooling and setting

175g (6oz) unsalted butter, softened, plus
  extra to grease

175g (6oz) caster sugar

3 medium eggs, lightly beaten

125g (4oz) self-raising flour

1 tsp baking powder

50g (2oz) ground almonds

1 tbsp milk

2 tbsp cocoa powder, sifted

For the icing

200g (7oz) plain chocolate, chopped

75g (3oz) unsalted butter

1 Preheat the oven to 190°C (170°C fan oven) mark 5. Grease a 900g (2lb) loaf tin and line with greaseproof paper, then grease the paper lightly.

2 Using a hand-held electric whisk, cream the butter and sugar together until pale and fluffy. Gradually add the eggs, beating well after each addition.

3 Sift the flour and baking powder into the bowl, then add the ground almonds and milk. Using a large metal spoon, fold everything together. Spoon half the mixture into a clean bowl and fold in the sifted cocoa powder.

4 Spoon a dollop of each mixture alternately into the prepared tin, until you have used up both mixtures. Tap the base of the tin once on a worksurface to level and remove any air bubbles. Draw a skewer backwards and forwards through the mixture a few times to create a marbled effect.

5 Bake for 45 minutes–1 hour until a skewer inserted into the centre comes out clean. Cool in the tin for 15 minutes, then turn out on to a wire rack (leave the lining paper on) and cool completely. When the cake is cold, peel off the lining paper and put the cake back on the wire rack.

6 To make the icing, melt the chocolate and butter in a heatproof bowl over a pan of gently simmering water, making sure the base of the bowl doesn't touch the water. Pour the chocolate icing over the cake and leave to set before serving. Serve in slices.

Cuts into 8 slices

Banana Cake

Hands-on time: 20 minutes
Cooking time: about 1 hour, plus cooling

125g (4oz) unsalted butter, softened, plus extra to grease

125g (4oz) light muscovado sugar

2 large eggs, lightly beaten

50g (2oz) smooth apple sauce

3 very ripe bananas, about 375g (13oz) peeled weight, mashed

1½ tsp mixed spice

150g (5oz) gluten-free plain flour blend

1 tsp gluten-free baking powder

a pinch of salt

For the icing

75g (3oz) unsalted butter, softened

100g (3½oz) icing sugar, sifted

50g (2oz) light muscovado sugar

½ tbsp milk (optional)

dried banana chips to decorate (optional)

1 Preheat the oven to 180°C (160°C fan oven) mark 4. Grease the base and sides of a 900g (2lb) loaf tin and line with baking parchment.

2 Using a hand-held electric whisk, beat the butter and muscovado sugar in a large bowl until pale and creamy. Gradually whisk in the eggs, then the apple sauce. Stir in the bananas.

3 Sift the spice, flour, baking powder and salt into the bowl, then use a large metal spoon to fold in (the mixture may look a little curdled). Spoon the mixture into the prepared tin.

4 Bake for 50 minutes–1 hour until risen and a skewer inserted into the centre comes out clean. Leave to cool in the tin for 10 minutes, then turn out on to a wire rack (leave the lining paper on) and leave to cool completely. When the cake is cold, remove the lining paper and put the cake on a serving plate.

5 To make the icing, whisk together the butter and both sugars until smooth. If needed, add a little milk to loosen. Spread over the top of the cooled cake. Decorate with banana chips, if you like. Serve in slices.

Cuts into 8-10 slices

Cappuccino and Walnut Cake

Hands-on time: 30 minutes
Cooking time: about 35 minutes, plus cooling

65g (2½oz) unsalted butter, melted and cooled, plus extra to grease

100g (3½oz) plain flour

1 tsp baking powder

4 medium eggs

125g (4oz) caster sugar

1 tbsp chicory and coffee essence

75g (3oz) walnuts, toasted, cooled and finely chopped

For the decoration

50g (2oz) walnuts

1 tbsp granulated sugar

¼ tsp ground cinnamon

For the icing

200g (7oz) white chocolate, chopped

4 tsp chicory and coffee essence

2 × 250g tubs mascarpone cheese

fresh unsprayed violets to decorate (optional)

1 Preheat the oven to 190°C (170°C fan oven) mark 5. Grease two 20.5 × 4cm (8 × 1½in) round cake tins and base-line each with a circle of greased greaseproof paper.

2 Sift the flour and baking powder together twice.

3 Using a hand-held electric whisk, beat the eggs and caster sugar in a large heatproof bowl over a pan of barely simmering water for 3–4 minutes until light, thick and fluffy. Take the bowl off the heat and continue whisking until the mixture has cooled and the whisk leaves a ribbon trail for 8 seconds when lifted out of the bowl.

4 Fold in the butter, coffee essence and chopped walnuts. Sift half the flour into the mixture and, using a metal spoon, fold it in carefully but quickly. Sift and fold in the rest of the flour, trying to knock out as little air as possible. Divide the mixture evenly between the prepared tins and tap them lightly on the worksurface.

5 Bake for 20–25 minutes until the cakes spring back when lightly pressed in the centre. Leave to cool in the tins for 10 minutes, then turn out on to a wire rack (leave the lining paper on) and leave to cool completely. When the cakes are cold, peel off the lining paper.

6 To make the decoration, whiz the walnuts with the granulated sugar and cinnamon in a food processor or blender until finely chopped. Take care not to over-process the nuts or they'll become oily. Put to one side.

7 To make the icing, melt the chocolate in a heatproof bowl over a pan of gently simmering water, making sure the base of the bowl doesn't touch the water. Allow to slowly melt without stirring. In another bowl, add the coffee essence to the mascarpone and beat until smooth, then slowly beat in the melted chocolate.

Cuts into 10 slices

8 Spread one-third of the icing on top of one cake, then sandwich with the other cake. Smooth the remaining icing over the top and sides. Lift the cake on to a large piece of greaseproof paper and scatter the chopped nuts all around it, then lift the greaseproof up to press the nuts on to the sides. Transfer to a plate and decorate with the violets, if you like. Serve in slices.

Cake Troubleshooting

Use this handy guide to help you find out where and why things might have gone wrong with your cake baking.

The cake sinks in the middle
- The oven door was opened too soon.
- The cake was under-baked.
- The ingredients haven't been measured accurately.
- The wrong size cake tin may have been used.

The cake has a cracked, domed top
- The oven temperature was too hot.
- The cake was too near the top of the oven.
- Insufficient liquid was used.
- The baking tin was too small.
- Too much raising agent was used.

The cake has a dense texture
- The mixture curdled when the eggs were being added.
- Too much liquid was used.
- The mixture was over-folded.
- Too little raising agent was used or an ineffective raising agent that was past its 'use-by date' was used.

The fruit has sunk to the bottom
- The mixture was too soft to support the weight of the fruit. This is liable to happen if the fruit was too sticky or wet.

The cake edges are crunchy
- The baking tin was over-greased.

Battenberg Delight

Hands-on time: 35 minutes
Cooking time: about 35 minutes, plus cooling

175g (6oz) unsalted butter, softened, plus extra to grease

175g (6oz) caster sugar

3 large eggs, lightly beaten

200g (7oz) self-raising flour

25g (1oz) ground almonds

a few drops of almond extract

pink and yellow food colouring

3–4 tbsp lemon curd

icing sugar to dust

500g (1lb 2oz) marzipan

1 Preheat the oven to 180°C (160°C fan oven) mark 4. Grease a 20.5cm (8in) square, straight-sided roasting/ brownie tin. Cut a rectangle of baking parchment that measures exactly 20.5 × 30.5cm (8 × 12in). Fold it in half (short end to short end), then make a fold 5cm (2in) wide down the length of the closed side, bending it both ways to mark a pleat. Open up the parchment, then pinch the pleat back together (so that it stands perpendicular to the rest of the parchment). Position the parchment in the bottom of the tin – it should line the bottom exactly and provide a 5cm (2in) divider down the middle.

2 Using a hand-held electric whisk, cream the butter and caster sugar together in a large bowl until pale and fluffy. Gradually beat in the eggs, then use a large metal spoon to fold in the flour, ground almonds and almond extract.

3 Spoon half the mixture into a separate bowl. Use the food colouring to tint one half yellow and the other pink. Spoon one batter into each side of the lined tin, making sure the parchment doesn't shift, and level the surface.

4 Bake for 30–35 minutes until a skewer inserted into the centre of each side comes out clean. Leave to cool in the tin.

5 When the cake is cold, turn out of the tin and peel off the lining paper. Using a bread knife, level the top of each cake and remove any browned

sponge. Stack the cakes and trim the sides and ends to reveal coloured sponge. With the sponges still stacked, halve the cakes lengthways to make four equal strips of sponge.

6 Spread a thin layer of lemon curd along one long side of a yellow strip, then stick it to a long side of a pink strip. Repeat with the remaining two strips. Stick the pairs of sponges on top of one another with more curd to give a chequerboard effect, then trim to neaten. Spread the ends of the cake with more curd.

7 Lightly dust the worksurface with icing sugar, then roll out one-eighth of the marzipan until 5mm (¼in) thick. Stick to one end of the cake and trim with scissors. Repeat with the other end.

8 Roll out the remaining marzipan into a long strip, 5mm (¼in) thick – it needs to be at least 22cm (8½in) wide and 35.5cm (14in) long. Brush with lemon curd. Place the cake on the marzipan at one of the short ends, then trim the width of the marzipan strip to match the cake. Roll the cake, sticking it to the marzipan as you go. Trim the end to neaten. Serve in slices.

Cuts into 10 slices

Dundee Cake

Hands-on time: 20 minutes
Cooking time: about 2 hours,
plus cooling

225g (8oz) unsalted butter or margarine,
softened, plus extra to grease

125g (4oz) currants

125g (4oz) raisins

50g (2oz) blanched almonds, chopped

125g (4oz) chopped mixed candied peel

300g (11oz) plain flour

225g (8oz) light muscovado sugar

finely grated zest of 1 lemon

4 large eggs, beaten

75g (3oz) split almonds to decorate

1 Preheat the oven to 170°C (150°C fan
oven) mark 3. Grease a deep 20.5cm
(8in) round cake tin and line with
greaseproof paper. Tie a double band
of brown paper around the outside
of the tin (to protect the cake from
burning while baking).

2 Combine the dried fruit, chopped nuts
and peel in a bowl. Sift in a little flour
and stir to coat the fruit.

3 Cream the butter and sugar together
in a bowl until pale and fluffy, then
beat in the lemon zest. Gradually beat
in the eggs, beating well after each
addition. Sift in the remaining flour
and, using a metal spoon, fold
in lightly, then fold in the fruit and
nut mixture.

4 Turn the mixture into the prepared
tin and, using the back of a metal
spoon, make a slight depression in
the middle of the surface of the cake
to ensure that it doesn't mound/dome
too much while baking. Arrange the
split almonds on top.

5 Bake on the middle shelf of the oven
for 2 hours or until a skewer inserted
into the centre comes out clean (if
necessary, cover the top of the cake
loosely with foil if it appears to be
browning too quickly). Leave to
cool in the tin for 15 minutes, then
turn out on to a wire rack (leave the
lining paper on) and leave to cool
completely. When the cake is cold,
wrap in greaseproof paper and foil
and leave to mature for at least a week
before cutting.

Cuts into 16 slices

Swiss Roll

Hands-on time: 25 minutes
Cooking time: about 12 minutes, plus cooling

unsalted butter to grease

125g (4oz) caster sugar, plus extra to dust

125g (4oz) plain flour, plus extra to dust

3 large eggs

For the filling and decoration

caster sugar

125g (4oz) jam, warmed

1 Preheat the oven to 200°C (180°C fan oven) mark 6. Grease and line a 33 × 23cm (13 × 9in) Swiss roll tin, then grease the paper lightly and dust with caster sugar and flour.

2 Put the eggs and sugar into a large, heatproof bowl and, using a hand-held electric whisk, beat until well combined. Put the bowl over a pan of hot water, making sure the base of the bowl doesn't touch the water, and whisk until the mixture is pale and creamy and thick enough to leave a trail on the surface when the whisk is lifted – this should take about

5 minutes. Remove the bowl from the pan and whisk until cool.

3 Sift half the flour over the mixture and, using a large metal spoon or spatula, fold it in very lightly. Sift in the remaining flour and gently fold in as before until combined. Carefully fold in 1 tbsp hot water.

4 Spoon the mixture into the prepared tin and tilt the tin to spread the mixture evenly. Bake for 10–12 minutes until pale golden, risen and springy to the touch.

5 Meanwhile, put a sheet of greaseproof paper larger than the Swiss roll tin on a damp teatowel. Dredge the paper with caster sugar. Quickly invert the cake on to the paper, then remove the tin and peel off the lining paper. If needed, trim off the crusty edges of the cake to neaten. Spread the jam over the top of the cake.

6 Using the greaseproof paper to help, roll up the cake from one of the short

ends. Make the first turn as tight as possible so that the cake will roll up evenly and have a good shape when finished. Once rolled, put seam-side down on a serving plate and sprinkle with caster sugar. Serve in slices.

Cuts into 8 slices

Serve It Up

To make a formal cake for a birthday, wedding or anniversary,
use the following chart to see the quantities of ingredients
required for your rich fruit cake, to fill the chosen cake tin or tins,
whether round or square.

SIZE	Size 1	Size 2	Size 3
SQUARE TIN SIZE	12.5cm (5in)	15cm (6in)	20.5cm (8in)
ROUND TIN SIZE	15cm (6in)	18cm (7in)	23cm (9in)
INGREDIENTS	225g (8oz) currants, 125g (4oz) each sultanas and raisins, 50g (2oz) glacé cherries, 25g (1oz) each mixed peel and flaked almonds, a little grated lemon zest, 175g (6oz) plain flour, ¼ tsp each mixed spice and cinnamon, 150g (5oz) each softened butter and soft brown sugar, 2½ medium eggs, beaten, 1 tbsp brandy	350g (12oz) currants, 125g (4oz) each sultanas and raisins, 75g (3oz) glacé cherries, 50g (2oz) each mixed peel and flaked almonds, a little grated lemon zest, 200g (7oz) plain flour, ½ tsp each mixed spice and cinnamon, 175g (6oz) each softened butter and soft brown sugar, 3 medium eggs, beaten, 1 tbsp brandy	625g (1lb 6oz) currants, 225g (8oz) each sultanas and raisins, 175g (6oz) glacé cherries, 125g (4oz) each mixed peel and flaked almonds, grated zest of ¼ lemon, 400g (14oz) plain flour, 1 tsp each mixed spice and cinnamon, 350g (12oz) each softened butter and soft brown sugar, 6 medium eggs, beaten, 2 tbsp brandy
ALMOND PASTE	350g (12oz)	450g (1lb)	800g (1¾lb)
ROYAL ICING	450g (1lb)	550g (1¼lb)	900g (2lb)

Note

When baking large cakes, 25.5cm (10in) and upwards, it is advisable to reduce the oven heat to 130°C (110°C fan oven) mark ½ after two-thirds of the cooking time. The amounts of Almond Paste quoted in this chart will give a thin covering. The quantities of Royal Icing should be enough for two coats. If using ready-to-roll fondant icing, use the quantities suggested for Royal Icing as a rough guide.

SIZE	Size 4	Size 5	Size 6
SQUARE TIN SIZE	23cm (9in)	28cm (11in)	30.5cm (12in)
ROUND TIN SIZE	25.5cm (10in)	30.5cm (12in)	33cm (13in)
INGREDIENTS	800g (1¾lb) currants, 375g (13oz) each sultanas and raisins, 250g (9oz) glacé cherries, 150g (5oz) each mixed peel and flaked almonds, zest of ¼–½ lemon, 600g (1lb 5oz) plain flour, 1 tsp each mixed spice and cinnamon, 500g (1lb 2oz) each softened butter and soft brown sugar, 9 medium eggs, beaten, 2–3 tbsp brandy	1.5kg (3lb 2oz) currants, 525g (1lb 3oz) each sultanas and raisins, 350g (12oz) glacé cherries, 250g (9oz) each mixed peel and flaked almonds, zest of ½ lemon, 825g (1lb 13oz) plain flour, 2½ tsp each mixed spice and cinnamon, 800g (1¾lb) each softened butter and soft brown sugar, 14 medium eggs, beaten, 4 tbsp brandy	1.7kg (3¾lb) currants, 625g (1lb 6oz) each sultanas and raisins, 425g (15oz) glacé cherries, 275g (10oz) each mixed peel and flaked almonds, zest of 1 lemon, 1kg (2¼lb) plain flour, 2½ tsp each mixed spice and cinnamon, 950g (2lb 2oz) each softened butter and soft brown sugar, 17 medium eggs, beaten, 6 tbsp brandy
ALMOND PASTE	900g (2lb)	1.1kg (2½lb)	1.4kg (3lb)
ROYAL ICING	1kg (2¼lb)	1.4kg (3lb)	1.6kg (3½lb)

Traditional Rich Fruit Cake

Hands-on time: 30 minutes, plus overnight soaking
Cooking time: about 3½ hours, plus cooling

450g (1lb) currants

200g (7oz) sultanas

200g (7oz) raisins

150g (5oz) glacé cherries

75g (3oz) chopped mixed peel

75g (3oz) flaked almonds

a little grated lemon zest

1 tbsp brandy

275g (10oz) unsalted butter, softened,
   plus extra to grease

350g (12oz) plain flour

½ tsp mixed spice

½ tsp ground cinnamon

275g (10oz) soft brown sugar

5 medium eggs, beaten

1 Put the currants, sultanas, raisins, glacé cherries, mixed peel, flaked almonds, lemon zest and brandy into a large, non-aluminium bowl (glass or ceramic is best, as this won't react with the fruit). Mix well, then cover with clingfilm and leave in a cool place to soak overnight.

2 When the fruit has soaked, grease a deep, 20.5cm (8in) round cake tin and line the base and sides with a double thickness of greaseproof paper. Grease the paper lightly. Tie a double band of brown paper around the outside of the tin (to protect the cake from burning while baking). Preheat the oven to 150°C (130°C fan oven) mark 2.

3 Sift the flour, mixed spice and cinnamon into a separate large bowl. Add the butter, sugar and eggs and, using a hand-held electric whisk, beat until smooth and glossy – this should take about 1 minute.

SAVE TIME

Store in an airtight container. It will keep for up to three months.

4 Using a large metal spoon or spatula, fold the soaked fruit into the flour mixture and continue folding until the fruit is evenly distributed. Spoon the mixture into the prepared tin and level the surface. Give the tin a few sharp taps on a worksurface to remove any air pockets. Using the back of a metal spoon, make a slight depression in the middle of the surface of the cake to ensure that it doesn't mound/dome too much while baking.

5 Put the tin on a baking sheet and cook in the middle of the oven for 3–3½ hours – cover the top with greaseproof paper after about 1½ hours – until the cake is firm to the touch and a skewer inserted into the centre comes out clean.

6 Leave to cool completely in the tin. When the cake is cold, turn out of the tin (leaving the lining paper around the cake). Wrap the cake in a double layer of greaseproof paper, then overwrap in a double layer of foil. Leave to mature for at least a week before cutting. Serve in slices.

Cuts into 16 large slices

Afternoon Tea Cakes

Deluxe Carrot Cake

Hands-on time: 30 minutes
Cooking time: about 1¾ hours, plus cooling

225ml (8fl oz) sunflower oil, plus extra
   to grease

225g (8oz) light muscovado sugar

4 medium eggs

225g (8oz) self-raising flour

1 tsp bicarbonate of soda

1½ tsp each mixed spice and
   ground cinnamon

1 orange

150g (5oz) sultanas

200g (7oz) carrots, peeled and
   coarsely grated

50g (2oz) walnuts, chopped

50g (2oz) preserved stem ginger,
   drained and chopped

For the frosting and decoration

600g (1lb 5oz) cream cheese

200g (7oz) icing sugar, sifted

finely grated zest of 1 orange

marzipan carrots
   (see opposite)

1 Preheat the oven to 170°C (150°C fan oven) mark 3. Grease the base and sides of a 20.5cm (8in) cake tin and line with baking parchment.

2 Whisk the oil, sugar and eggs in a large bowl until smooth. Stir in the flour, bicarbonate of soda and spices. Finely grate the zest of the orange and add to the mixture with the juice from only half the orange. Add the sultanas, carrots, walnuts and ginger and mix well. Spoon the mixture into the prepared tin.

3 Bake for 30 minutes, then cover the top of the cake loosely with foil and bake for a further 1¼ hours or until a skewer inserted into the centre comes out clean. Leave to cool in the tin for 5 minutes, then turn out on to a wire rack (leave the lining paper on) and leave to cool completely. When the cake is cold, peel off the lining paper and cut the cake in two horizontally.

4 To make the frosting, mix the cream cheese, icing sugar and orange zest in a bowl. Use half the frosting to sandwich the two cake halves together. Spread the remaining frosting over the top and decorate with marzipan carrots.

To make marzipan carrots

Colour 75g (3oz) marzipan with orange food colouring and 15g (½oz) marzipan with green food colouring. Divide the orange marzipan into 12 pieces, then shape each piece into a cone. Using a cocktail stick, mark on ridges. Divide the green marzipan into 12 pieces, then shape each piece into a frond to resemble leaves and stick on to the carrots.

SAVE TIME

Store in an airtight container. It will keep for up to two days. Alternatively, the cake will keep for up to one week in an airtight container if it is stored before the frosting is applied.

Cuts into 12 slices

Lemon and Poppy Seed Buttermilk Cake

Hands-on time: 25 minutes
Cooking time: about 40 minutes, plus cooling

150g (5oz) unsalted butter, softened, plus extra to grease

175g (6oz) granulated sugar

3 large eggs, lightly beaten

finely grated zest and juice of 2 lemons

1 tsp vanilla extract

125g (4oz) buttermilk

1 tbsp poppy seeds

250g (9oz) plain flour

2 tsp baking powder

For the icing

150g (5oz) full-fat cream cheese, at room temperature

75g (3oz) unsalted butter, softened

2 tbsp lemon curd

350g (12oz) icing sugar, sifted

crystallized rose petals (optional)

1 Preheat the oven to 180°C (160°C fan oven) mark 4. Lightly grease a 20.5cm (8in) round cake tin and line with baking parchment.

2 Put the butter and granulated sugar into a large bowl and, using a hand-held electric whisk, cream together until pale and fluffy – this should take about 3 minutes. Gradually beat in the eggs, mixing constantly, followed by the lemon zest and juice, vanilla extract, buttermilk and poppy seeds.

3 Sift the flour and baking powder into the bowl, then use a large metal spoon to fold it in. Spoon the mixture into the prepared tin.

4 Bake for 40 minutes or until a skewer inserted into the centre comes out clean. Leave to cool in the tin for 5 minutes, then turn out on to a wire rack (leave the lining paper on) and leave to cool completely. When

the cake is cold, peel off the lining paper and transfer to a cake stand or serving plate.

5 To make the icing, put the cream cheese, softened butter and lemon curd into a food processor and whiz together until smooth (alternatively, whisk together by hand). Add the icing sugar and whiz again to combine. Spread over the top of the cake and decorate with crystallized rose petals, if you like.

Cuts into 10 slices

Spiced Pecan, Apple and Cranberry Cake

Hands-on time: 20 minutes
Cooking time: about 1 hour, plus cooling

175g (6oz) unsalted butter, softened, plus extra to grease

150g (5oz) caster sugar

3 medium eggs

1 tsp vanilla extract

150g (5oz) plain flour

1 tsp baking powder

2 tbsp milk

½ tsp ground cinnamon

3 Braeburn apples, peeled, cored and cut into 1cm (½in) cubes

50g (2oz) fresh cranberries, thawed if frozen

75g (3oz) pecan nuts, roughly chopped

2–3 tbsp apricot jam

1 Preheat the oven to 180°C (160°C fan oven) mark 4. Grease a 20.5cm (8in) springform cake tin and line with baking parchment.

2 Using a freestanding mixer or hand-held electric whisk, beat 150g (5oz) butter with the sugar, eggs, vanilla extract, flour, baking powder and milk until pale and fluffy – this should take about 5 minutes. Spoon into the prepared tin and level the surface. Bake for 10 minutes.

3 Meanwhile, heat the remaining butter in a large frying pan until foaming. Stir in the cinnamon and apples and cook for 3 minutes until almost tender. Take off the heat and stir in the cranberries and pecan nuts.

4 Carefully take the part-baked cake out of the oven and sprinkle the apple mixture over the surface. Return to the oven and bake for a further 40–50 minutes until a skewer inserted into the centre comes out clean.

5 Leave to cool in the tin for 5 minutes, then turn out of the tin and peel off the lining paper. Transfer to a serving plate. Gently warm the jam in a small pan to loosen, then brush over the top of the cake. Serve the cake warm or at room temperature.

Cuts into 8 slices

Take 5 Tins

Unless otherwise stated, line your tins with greaseproof paper (use baking parchment for roulades or meringues). This will help stop the cake sticking to the sides of the tin or burning. Lightly grease the inside of the tin first to help keep the paper in place. Apply the butter or oil with kitchen paper – do not thickly grease the edges of the cake tin, you need just enough to hold the paper in place. Once the tin is lined, grease the paper lightly.

Lining a loaf tin

1 Cut out a sheet of greaseproof paper the same length as the base of the tin and wide enough to cover both the base and the long sides. Now cut another sheet to the same width as the base and long enough to cover both the base and the ends of the tin.

2 Lightly grease the inside of the tin with butter. Press the strips into position, making sure they fit snugly into the corners. Lightly grease with butter.

2

Lining a square tin

This method works well for larger square tins. For small tins, rather than cutting four side panels, use one long strip.

1 Put the tin base-down on greaseproof paper and draw around it. Cut out the square just inside the drawn line. Next, measure the length and depth of one of the sides of the tin. Cut four strips of greaseproof paper to this length, each about 2cm (¾in) wider than the depth of the tin. Fold up one of the long edges of each strip by 1cm (½in).

2 Lightly grease the inside of the tin with butter. Position the four strips in the tin, with the folded edge lying on the bottom. Next, lay the square on the bottom of the tin, then lightly grease the paper, taking care not to move the side strips.

Lining a round tin

1. Put the tin base-down on greaseproof paper and draw a circle around its circumference. Cut out the circle just inside the drawn line.
2. Cut a long strip about 2cm (¾in) wider than the depth of the tin, and long enough to wrap around the outside of the tin. Fold up one long edge of the strip by 1cm (½in). Make cuts, spacing them about 2.5cm (1in) apart, through the folded edge of the strip(s) up to the fold line.
3. Lightly grease the inside of the tin with butter. Press the strip to the inside of the tin, making sure the snipped edges sit on the bottom. Trim any overlap once inside the tin.
4. Lay the circle in the bottom of the tin, then lightly grease the paper, taking care not to move the side strips.

3

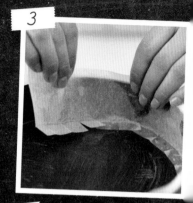

4

Lining a Swiss roll tin

Use this method for a Swiss roll or any other shallow baking tin.

1 Put the tin base-down in the centre of a large sheet of greaseproof paper or baking parchment and trim the paper so that it is 2.5cm (1in) wider than the tin on all sides. Still with the tin on the paper, cut from one corner of the paper to the closest corner of the tin. Repeat with the remaining corners.
2 Lightly grease the inside of the tin with butter. Fit the paper into the tin, neatly pressing into the corners. Lightly grease the paper.

Lining shaped tins

1 Put the tin base-down on greaseproof paper. Draw around the base following the tin shape and cut out.
2 Measure and cut a strip of greaseproof paper to fit around the outside of the tin. Lightly grease the inside of the tin with butter, then line the base and sides with the paper and grease again.

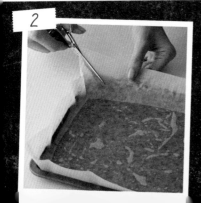

Lemon Drizzle Loaf

Hands-on time: 20 minutes
Cooking time: about 50 minutes, plus cooling

175g (6oz) unsalted butter, softened, plus extra to grease

175g (6oz) caster sugar

4 medium eggs, lightly beaten

3 lemons

125g (4oz) self-raising flour

50g (2oz) ground almonds

75g (3oz) sugar cubes

1 Preheat the oven to 180°C (160°C fan oven) mark 4. Grease a 900g (2lb) loaf tin and line with baking parchment.

2 Put the butter and caster sugar into a large bowl and, using a hand-held electric whisk, cream together until pale and fluffy – this should take about 5 minutes. Gradually beat in the eggs, followed by the finely grated zest of 2 of the lemons and the juice of ½ a lemon. Fold the flour and ground almonds into the butter mixture, then spoon into the prepared tin.

3 Bake for 40–50 minutes until a skewer inserted into the centre comes out clean. Leave to cool in the tin for 10 minutes, then turn out, peel off the lining paper and leave to cool on a wire rack until just warm.

4 Meanwhile, put the sugar cubes into a small bowl with the juice of 1½ lemons and the pared zest of 1 lemon (you should have 1 un-juiced lemon left over). Soak for 5 minutes, then use the back of a spoon to roughly crush the cubes. Spoon over the warm cake and leave to cool completely before serving in slices.

SAVE TIME

Store in an airtight container. It will keep for up to four days.

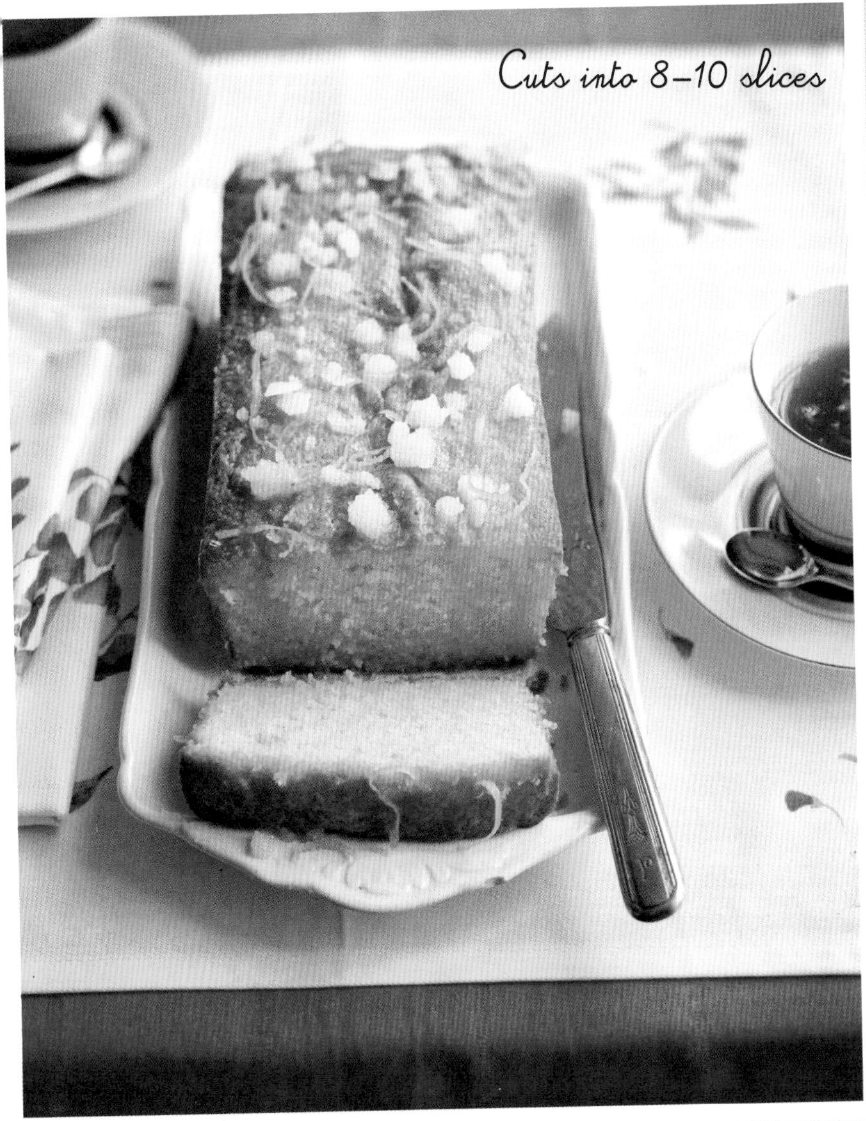
Cuts into 8–10 slices

Fruity Teacake

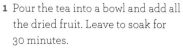

Gluten Free

Hands-on time: 20 minutes, plus soaking
Cooking time: 1 hour, plus cooling

150ml (¼ pint) hot black tea, made with
  2 Earl Grey tea bags

200g (7oz) sultanas

75g (3oz) ready-to-eat dried figs,
  roughly chopped

75g (3oz) ready-to-eat dried prunes,
  roughly chopped

a little vegetable oil

125g (4oz) dark muscovado sugar

2 medium eggs, beaten

225g (8oz) gluten-free flour

2 tsp wheat-free baking powder

2 tsp ground mixed spice

butter to serve (optional)

1 Pour the tea into a bowl and add all
  the dried fruit. Leave to soak for
  30 minutes.

2 Preheat the oven to 190°C (170°C fan
  oven) mark 5. Grease a 900g (2lb)
  loaf tin and base-line with
  greaseproof paper.

3 Beat the sugar and eggs together in
  a large bowl until pale and slightly
  thickened. Add the flour, baking
  powder, mixed spice and soaked dried
  fruit and tea, then mix together well.
  Spoon the mixture into the prepared
  tin and level the surface.

4 Bake on the middle shelf of the oven
  for 45 minutes–1 hour. Leave to cool
  completely in the tin. When the cake
  is cold, turn out and peel off the lining
  paper. Serve sliced, with a little butter
  if you like.

SAVE TIME

Wrap in clingfilm and store in an
airtight container. It will keep for up
to five days.

Cuts into 12 slices

Honey and Spice Loaf Cake

Hands-on time: 20 minutes
Cooking time: about 55 minutes, plus cooling and setting

2 tbsp runny honey

200g (7oz) unsalted butter

80g (3¼oz) dark soft brown sugar

2 large eggs

200g (7oz) self-raising flour

1½ tsp mixed spice

100g (3½oz) icing sugar, sifted

butter to serve (optional)

1 Put the honey, butter and brown sugar into a pan and melt together over a low heat. When the sugar has dissolved, turn up the heat and leave to bubble for 1 minute. Take off the heat and leave to cool for 15 minutes.

2 Preheat the oven to 160°C (140°C fan oven) mark 3. Line a 900g (2lb) loaf tin with baking parchment.

3 Mix the eggs into the melted butter. Sift the flour and mixed spice into a large bowl and add the butter mixture. Mix well, then pour into the prepared tin.

4 Bake for 40-50 minutes until a skewer inserted into the centre comes out clean. Leave to cool in the tin for 5 minutes, then turn out on to a wire rack (leave the lining paper on) and leave to cool completely. When the cake is cold, peel off the lining paper and put the cake on a serving plate.

5 To make the glaze, put the icing sugar into a bowl and whisk in just enough water to get a runny consistency. Drizzle over the cake and leave to harden a little. Serve in slices, spread with butter if you like.

Cuts into 8 slices

Orange and Apricot Tea Loaf

Hands-on time: 15 minutes
Cooking time: about 1¼ hours, plus cooling

175g (6oz) unsalted butter, softened, plus extra to grease

175g (6oz) light soft brown sugar

3 large eggs, lightly beaten

200g (7oz) plain flour

1 tsp baking powder

100g (3½oz) mixed peel

100g (3½oz) finely chopped apricots

50g (2oz) walnuts, chopped

grated zest of 1 large orange

butter to serve (optional)

To glaze

2 tbsp marmalade

1 tbsp runny honey

1 Preheat the oven to 170°C (150°C fan oven) mark 3. Lightly grease a 900g (2lb) loaf tin and line with baking parchment.

2 Put the butter and sugar into a bowl and, using a hand-held electric whisk, cream together until pale and fluffy. Gradually beat in the eggs.

3 Sift the flour and baking powder into the bowl, then use a large metal spoon to fold in. Stir in the dried fruit, walnuts and half the orange zest. Spoon the mixture into the prepared tin.

4 Bake for 1 hour–1 hour 10 minutes until a skewer inserted into the centre comes out clean (if necessary, cover the top of the cake loosely with foil if it appears to be browning too quickly). Leave to cool in the tin for 5 minutes, then turn out on to a wire rack (leave the lining paper on) and leave to cool completely. When the cake is cold, peel off the lining paper and put the cake on a serving plate.

5 To make the glaze, put the marmalade and honey into a small pan and heat gently until runny. Drizzle over the cooled cake and sprinkle the remaining orange zest on top. Serve in slices, spread with butter if you like.

Cuts into 10 slices

Test it, Store It

Ovens vary and the time given in the recipe might be too short or too long to correctly cook what you are baking. So always test to ensure a successful result.

Testing sponges

1. Gently press the centre of the sponge. It should feel springy. If it's a whisked cake, it should be just shrinking away from the sides of the tin.
2. If you have to put it back into the oven, close the door gently so that the vibrations don't cause the cake to sink in the centre.

Testing fruit cakes

1 To test if a fruit cake is cooked, insert a skewer into the centre of the cake, leave for a few moments, then pull it out. If it comes away clean, the cake is ready.

2 If any mixture sticks to the skewer, the cake is not quite done, so put the cake back in the oven for a few more minutes, then test again with a clean skewer.

Cooling cakes

Always follow the cooling instructions stated in the recipe. If certain cakes are left for too long in the tin, they will sweat. Most rich

Storing cakes

With the exception of rich fruit cakes and gingerbread, most cakes are best enjoyed freshly baked. If storing is necessary, use a cake tin or large plastic container. Make sure that the cake is completely cold before you put it into the container. If you haven't a large enough container, wrap the cake in a double layer of greaseproof paper and overwrap with foil. Avoid putting rich fruit cakes in direct contact with foil – the fruit may react with it. Never store a cake in the same tin as biscuits, as the biscuits will quickly soften.

Most cakes, particularly sponges, freeze well, but they are generally best frozen before filling and decorating. If freezing a finished gateau, open-freeze first, then pack in a rigid container.

Almond and Apricot Cake

Hands-on time: 15 minutes
Cooking time: 15 minutes, plus cooling

175g (6oz) unsalted butter, softened, plus
    extra to grease

125g (4oz) caster sugar

4 medium eggs

175g (6oz) self-raising flour

75g (3oz) ground almonds

finely grated zest and juice of 1 lemon

For the filling

250g tub mascarpone cheese

40g (1½oz) icing sugar, plus extra to dust

4 tbsp apricot compote

1 Preheat the oven to 200°C (180°C fan oven) mark 6. Grease two 18cm (7in) round sandwich tins and line with greaseproof paper.

2 Beat the butter and caster sugar together until fluffy, then beat in the eggs, one at a time, until combined. Using a metal spoon, gently fold in the flour, ground almonds, lemon zest and juice and stir until smooth. Divide the mixture equally between the prepared tins and level the surface.

3 Bake for 15 minutes or until golden and a skewer inserted into the centre comes out clean. Leave to cool in the tins for 5 minutes, then turn out on to a wire rack (leave the lining paper on) and leave to cool completely. When the cakes are cold, peel off the lining paper.

4 To make the filling, beat the mascarpone and icing sugar together in a bowl. Spread over one of the cakes. Spoon the apricot compote evenly over the cheese mixture and put the other cake on top. Dust with icing sugar and cut into slices to serve.

Cuts into 12 slices

Raspberry and Peach Cake

Hands-on time: 15 minutes
Cooking time: about 1¼ hours, plus cooling

200g (7oz) unsalted butter, melted plus extra to grease

250g (9oz) self-raising flour, sifted

175g (6oz) light muscovado sugar

4 medium eggs, beaten

125g (4oz) raspberries

3 large almost-ripe peaches or nectarines, halved, stoned and diced

4 tbsp apricot jam

juice of ½ lemon

1 Preheat the oven to 190°C (170°C fan oven) mark 5. Grease a 20.5cm (8in) springform cake tin and base-line with baking parchment.

2 Put the flour and sugar into a large bowl and make a well in the centre. Add the melted butter and the eggs and mix well.

3 Spread half the mixture over the bottom of the prepared tin and add half the raspberries and sliced peaches or nectarines. Spoon the remaining cake mixture over the top and smooth over, then add the remaining raspberries and peaches or nectarines, pressing them down into the mixture slightly.

4 Bake for 1–1¼ hours until risen and golden and a skewer inserted into the centre comes out clean. Remove from the oven and leave to cool in the tin for 10 minutes. Turn out of the tin, peel off the lining paper and place the cake on a serving plate..

5 Warm the jam and lemon juice together in a small pan and brush over the cake to glaze. Serve warm or at room temperature.

Cuts into 8 slices

Sticky Lemon Polenta Cake

Hands-on time: 10 minutes
Cooking time: 1 hour, plus cooling

50g (2oz) unsalted butter, softened, plus extra to grease

3 lemons

250g (9oz) golden caster sugar

250g (9oz) instant polenta

1 tsp baking powder

2 large eggs

50ml (2fl oz) semi-skimmed milk

2 tbsp natural yogurt

2 tbsp poppy seeds

---

1 Preheat the oven to 180°C (160°C fan oven) mark 4. Lightly grease a 900g (2lb) loaf tin and base-line with greaseproof paper.

2 Grate the zest of 1 lemon and put into a food processor with the butter, 200g (7oz) sugar, the polenta, baking powder, eggs, milk, yogurt and poppy seeds, then whiz until smooth. Spoon the mixture into the prepared tin and level the surface.

3 Bake for 55 minutes–1 hour until a skewer inserted into the centre comes out clean. Leave to cool in the tin for 10 minutes.

4 Next, make a syrup. Squeeze the juice from the zested lemon plus 1 more lemon. Thinly slice the third lemon. Put the lemon juice into a pan with the remaining sugar and 150ml (¼ pint) water. Add the lemon slices, bring to the boil and bubble for about 10 minutes until syrupy. Take the pan off the heat and leave to cool for 5 minutes. Remove the lemon slices from the syrup and put to one side.

5 Slide a knife around the edge of the cake and turn out on to a serving plate. Remove the lining paper. Pierce the cake in several places with a skewer, spoon the syrup over it and decorate with the lemon slices.

Wrap in clingfilm and store in an airtight container. It will keep for up to three days.

Cuts into 12 slices

Courgette Cake

150ml (¼ pint) vegetable oil, plus extra
   to grease

250g (9oz) self-raising flour, plus extra
   to dust

50g (2oz) pistachios (shelled weight)

3 medium eggs

175g (6oz) caster sugar

1 tsp vanilla extract

½ tsp bicarbonate of soda

2 small courgettes, about 225g (8oz),
   coarsely grated

For the icing

125g (4oz) icing sugar, sifted

1 tbsp roughly chopped pistachios

SAVE EFFORT

This cake can also be made in a
deep 20.5cm (8in) round cake tin.
Follow the recipe, baking the cake
for about 55 minutes.

1 Preheat the oven to 180°C (160°C fan oven) mark 4. Grease a 25.5cm (10in) kugelhopf or bundt tin. Lightly dust with flour and tap out the excess. Pulse the pistachios in a food processor until finely ground (or chop by hand), then put to one side.

2 Whisk the oil, eggs, sugar and vanilla extract together in a large bowl. Sift in the flour and bicarbonate of soda and stir to combine. Mix in the courgettes and pistachios. Tip into the prepared tin and level the surface.

3 Bake for 35 minutes or until golden and a skewer inserted into the centre comes out clean. Leave to cool in the tin for 5 minutes, then turn out on to a wire rack and leave to cool completely.

4 To make the icing, mix the icing sugar with enough water (1½–2 tbsp) to get a smooth, fairly thick icing. Slide the cake on to a cake stand or serving plate. Drizzle the icing over it, then scatter the chopped pistachios on top. Serve in slices.

Oven Scones

Hands-on time: 15 minutes
Cooking time: 10 minutes, plus cooling

40g (1½oz) unsalted butter, diced, plus extra to grease

225g (8oz) self-raising flour, plus extra to dust

a pinch of salt

1 tsp baking powder

about 150ml (¼ pint) milk

beaten egg or milk to glaze

whipped cream, or butter and jam to serve

SAVE EFFORT

To ensure a good rise, avoid heavy handling and make sure that the rolled-out dough is at least 2cm (¾in) thick.

1 Preheat the oven to 220°C (200°C fan oven) mark 7. Grease a baking sheet.

2 Sift the flour, salt and baking powder into a bowl. Rub in the butter until the mixture resembles fine breadcrumbs. Using a knife to stir it in, add enough milk to give a fairly soft dough.

3 Gently roll or pat out the dough on a lightly floured worksurface to a 2cm (¾in) thickness and then, using a 6.5cm (2½in) plain cutter, cut out rounds. Put on the baking sheet and brush the tops with beaten egg or milk.

4 Bake for about 10 minutes until golden brown and well risen. Transfer to a wire rack and leave to cool.

5 Serve warm, split and filled with cream, or spread with butter and jam.

Makes 8

Crumpets

Hands-on time: 20 minutes, plus rising
Cooking time: about 35 minutes

350g (12oz) strong plain white flour
½ tsp salt
½ tsp bicarbonate of soda
1½ tsp fast-action dried yeast
250ml (9fl oz) warm milk
a little vegetable oil to fry
butter to serve

1 Sift the flour, salt and bicarbonate of soda into a large bowl and stir in the yeast. Make a well in the centre, then pour in 300ml (½ pint) warm water and the milk. Mix to a thick batter.

2 Using a wooden spoon, beat the batter vigorously for about 5 minutes. Cover and leave in a warm place for about 1 hour until sponge-like in texture. Beat the batter for a further 2 minutes, then transfer to a jug.

3 Put a large, non-stick frying pan over a high heat and brush a little oil over the surface. Oil the insides of four crumpet rings or 7.5cm (3in) plain metal cutters. Put the rings, blunt-edge down, on the hot pan's surface and leave for about 2 minutes until very hot.

4 Pour a little batter into each ring to a depth of 1cm (½in). Cook the crumpets for 4–5 minutes until the surface is set and appears honeycombed with holes.

5 Carefully remove each metal ring. Flip the crumpets over and cook the other side for 1 minute only. Transfer to a wire rack. Repeat to use all of the batter.

6 To serve, toast the crumpets on both sides and serve with butter.

Makes about 24

Cupcakes

Sticky Gingerbread Cupcakes

Hands-on time: 35 minutes
Cooking time: 20 minutes, plus cooling

175g (6oz) self-raising flour

75g (3oz) unsalted butter, chilled and cut into cubes

¼ tsp bicarbonate of soda

2 tsp ground ginger

25g (1oz) preserved stem ginger, drained and finely chopped, plus 3 tbsp syrup from the jar

50g (2oz) dark muscovado sugar

50g (2oz) golden syrup

50g (2oz) treacle

juice of 1 orange

2 medium eggs, beaten

For the topping and decoration

100g (3½oz) unsalted butter, softened

200g (7oz) icing sugar, sifted

3 tbsp syrup from the stem ginger jar

1 tsp ground ginger

ready-made sugar flowers (optional)

1 Preheat the oven to 190°C (170°C fan oven) mark 5. Line a 12-hole muffin tin with nine paper muffin cases.

2 Put the flour into a large bowl. Using your fingertips, rub in the butter until it resembles breadcrumbs. Stir in the bicarbonate of soda, ground ginger and stem ginger and put to one side. Put the muscovado sugar, golden syrup, treacle and orange juice into a small pan and heat gently until the sugar dissolves. Cool for 5 minutes.

3 Mix the eggs and warm sugar mixture into the flour mixture and stir with a spatula until just combined. Spoon the mixture equally into the paper cases.

4 Bake for 20 minutes or until golden and risen. Remove from the oven. Drizzle each cake with 1 tsp ginger syrup. Leave to cool in the tin for 5 minutes, then transfer to a wire rack and leave to cool completely.

5 To make the buttercream topping, put the butter into a bowl and whisk until fluffy. Add the icing sugar, ginger

syrup and ground ginger and whisk until light and fluffy. Using a palette knife, spread a little buttercream over the top of each cake. Decorate with sugar flowers, if you like.

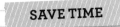

SAVE TIME

Store in an airtight container. They will keep for three to five days.

Makes 9

Tropical Burst Cupcakes

Hands-on time: 35 minutes
Cooking time: 20 minutes, plus cooling and setting

200g (7oz) self-raising flour, sifted

½ tsp bicarbonate of soda

100g (3½oz) caster sugar

50g (2oz) ready-to-eat dried tropical
   fruit, finely chopped

3 medium eggs

100ml (3½fl oz) sunflower oil

75ml (2½fl oz) buttermilk

1 × 227g can pineapple pieces, drained
   and finely chopped

For the topping and decoration

225g (8oz) royal icing sugar, sifted

grated zest and juice of 1 lime

sugar decorations (optional)

1 Preheat the oven to 190°C (170°C fan oven) mark 5. Line a 12-hole muffin tin with paper muffin cases.

2 Put the flour, bicarbonate of soda, caster sugar and dried fruit into a large bowl. Put the eggs, oil and buttermilk into a jug and lightly beat together until combined. Pour the oil mixture and the pineapple pieces into the flour mixture and stir with a spatula until just combined. Spoon the mixture equally into the paper cases.

3 Bake for 20 minutes or until lightly golden and risen. Leave to cool in the tin for 5 minutes, then transfer to a wire rack and leave to cool completely.

4 To make the topping, put the icing sugar, lime juice and zest and 1 tbsp cold water into a bowl and whisk for 5 minutes or until soft peaks form. Using a small palette knife, spread a little over the top of each cake. Stand the cakes on the wire rack, scatter with sugar decorations, if you like, and leave for about 1 hour to set.

Makes 12

Coconut and Lime Cupcakes

Hands-on time: 30 minutes
Cooking time: about 20 minutes, plus cooling and setting

275g (10oz) plain flour, sifted

1 tbsp baking powder

100g (3½oz) caster sugar

grated zest of 1 lime

50g (2oz) desiccated coconut

2 medium eggs

100ml (3½fl oz) sunflower oil

225g (8oz) natural yogurt

50ml (2fl oz) milk

For the topping

150g (5oz) icing sugar, sifted

juice of 1 lime

50g (2oz) desiccated coconut

1 Preheat the oven to 200°C (180°C fan oven) mark 6. Line a 12-hole muffin tin with paper muffin cases.

2 Put the flour, baking powder, caster sugar, lime zest and coconut into a large bowl. Put the eggs, oil, yogurt and milk into a jug and lightly beat together until combined.

3 Pour the yogurt mixture into the flour mixture and stir with a spatula until just combined. Spoon the mixture equally into the paper cases.

4 Bake for 18–20 minutes until lightly golden and risen. Leave to cool in the tin for 5 minutes, then transfer to a wire rack and leave to cool completely.

5 To make the topping, mix the icing sugar with the lime juice and 1–2 tsp boiling water to make a thick, smooth icing. Put the coconut into a shallow bowl. Dip the top of each cake into the icing until coated, allowing the excess to drip off, then carefully dip into the coconut until coated. Stand the cakes on the wire rack and leave for about 1 hour to set.

There has been quite a revolution in the food colouring industry over the past few years. Nearly gone are the watery liquids in a limited range of colours that dilute the mediums we were trying to colour, rather than tint them. These have been replaced with a range of vibrant pastes, powders and concentrated liquid colours and pens. Visit a specialist cake shop or website, as there are so many great products to help you create stunning cake designs.

Liquid colours

Liquid colours tend to be cheaper and more suitable for adding to cake mixes than to icing. Add drop by drop to achieve the desired colour – but care must be taken, as they can easily dilute the mixtures (and can cause mixtures to curdle if too much is added). They are available from most supermarkets in a wide range of everyday colours.

Paste colours

These very concentrated moist pastes come in every possible colour you can need. They are ideal for colouring buttercream, sugarpaste and royal icing, as well as flower paste and marzipan. They are so concentrated that they will not affect the consistency of the mixture regardless of the depth of colour required. Apply with a cocktail stick a dot at a time until you have reached the desired shade. The pastes can also be applied neat with a paintbrush to add fine definition to work. When colouring with dark food colouring pastes, the colour can deepen on standing. Ideally (if using dark shades), tint to a shade lighter than the ultimate desired shade, then cover the icing/marzipan and leave to stand for 2–3 hours before using.

Colour dusts

These edible powdered food colourings are suitable for kneading into sugarpaste, brushing to add colour to finished decorations, or for shading and colouring base icings on cakes. Dip a brush into the dust, then work the brush into or over the icing. A vast range of colours is available.

Food colouring pens

These pens are filled with a variety of liquid food colourings. Their consistency can be a little unreliable when writing on sugarpaste, royal icing or marzipan, but when used to add small colour accents to sugarcraft they can be useful.

Lustre colours

These edible food colourings come in different powdered finishes – pearl, iridescent, metallic and sparkle. They give subtle colour with a high-sheen finish and are non-water soluble. The real advantage of these lustre colours is that they can be brushed on to dried decorations that have been made out of white sugar or flower paste. Different colours and shades may be applied to give a realistic effect.

SAVE EFFORT

Try stencilling food colouring dusts on to the surface of a sugarpasted cake. Dampen a sponge or piece of muslin and wring out well. Scrunch it up and dab quickly into the food dust. Lightly dab the surface of the sugarpaste to imprint the colour. Re-dip into the colour as necessary. Always practise on an unwanted scrap of sugarpaste first to achieve the desired technique.

The Ultimate Carrot Cupcakes

Hands-on time: 30 minutes
Cooking time: 20 minutes, plus cooling

150g (5oz) carrots, peeled and
   coarsely grated

50g (2oz) raisins

175g (6oz) self-raising flour, sifted

½ tsp bicarbonate of soda

150g (5oz) light soft brown sugar

grated zest of 1 orange

½ tsp ground mixed spice

3 medium eggs

100ml (3½fl oz) sunflower oil

75ml (2½fl oz) buttermilk

For the topping and decoration

50g (2oz) icing sugar, sifted

250g (9oz) mascarpone cheese

100g (3½oz) quark cheese

juice of ½ orange

red, yellow and green sugarpaste
   (optional)

1 Preheat the oven to 190°C (170°C fan oven) mark 5. Line a 12-hole muffin tin with paper muffin cases.

2 Put the carrots into a large bowl and add the raisins, flour, bicarbonate of soda, brown sugar, orange zest and mixed spice. Put the eggs, oil and buttermilk into a jug and lightly beat together until combined. Pour the egg mixture into the flour mixture and stir with a spatula until just combined. Spoon the mixture equally into the paper cases.

3 Bake for 20 minutes or until lightly golden and risen. Cool in the tin for 5 minutes, then transfer to a wire rack and leave to cool completely.

4 To make the topping, mix the icing sugar with the mascarpone, quark and orange juice to a smooth icing. Using a small palette knife, spread a little of the icing over each cake. Use the coloured sugarpaste to make small carrots, if you like, and decorate the cakes with them.

Lemon and Vanilla Cupcakes

Hands-on time: 25 minutes
Cooking time: about 15 minutes, plus cooling

200g (7oz) golden caster sugar

200g (7oz) unsalted butter, very soft

finely grated zest and juice of 1 lemon

4 medium eggs, beaten

200g (7oz) self-raising flour

For the icing and decoration

75g (3oz) unsalted butter, softened

175g (6oz) icing sugar, sifted

1–2 tbsp milk

1 tsp vanilla extract

selection of sugar sprinkles

1 Preheat the oven to 200°C (180°C fan oven) mark 6. Line a 12-hole muffin tin with paper muffin cases.

2 Put the caster sugar, butter and lemon zest into a large bowl. Using a hand-held electric whisk, beat together, or beat with a wooden spoon, until pale and creamy. Beat in the eggs, a little at a time, folding in 1 tbsp flour if the mixture looks as if it's about to curdle.

3 Using a metal spoon, fold in the remaining flour and lemon juice. Spoon the mixture equally into the paper cases.

4 Bake for 12–15 minutes until golden. Leave to cool in the tin for 5 minutes, then transfer to a wire rack and leave to cool completely.

5 To make the icing, put the butter into a large bowl and, using a hand-held electric whisk, beat in two-thirds of the icing sugar. Gradually beat in the rest of the icing sugar with the milk and vanilla extract until you have a soft but spreadable consistency that holds a shape.

6 Using a small palette knife, spread a little of the icing over each cake and swirl with the knife to form peaks. Decorate with sugar sprinkles.

Makes 12

The icing or topping on cupcakes is now almost as important as the cake underneath. Icing helps keep the cake softer for longer (as long as the cakes are kept in their paper cases) and allows you to theme and decorate your cupcakes as desired.

Piping icing on to cupcakes

Many cupcake bakeries have developed a signature swirl of buttercream icing – practise and soon you'll have your own. Half-fill the piping bag with buttercream or frosting and hold the bag vertically as you pipe, squeezing gently from the top.

Spreading

Start by gently brushing the top of the cooled cupcake with your finger or a brush to remove crumbs. Dollop a generous amount of buttercream or frosting on to the cake (it takes more than you might think) and gently spread it to the sides of the cake with a palette or butter knife for a smooth look. Alternatively, push the icing or frosting into a swirl or points with your spatula or knife.

Filling cupcakes

Before icing it, you can easily fill your cupcake with extra icing, buttercream or smooth jam. Insert a plain nozzle (not too fine) into a piping bag, half-fill the bag with the chosen filling and push the nozzle down through the top into the centre of the un-iced cake (alternatively, hollow out some of the cake with a small knife first). Squeeze in some mixture, then ice as normal. It's worth cutting your first filled cake in half vertically to check how much filling you have managed to get into the cupcake.

Flooding cupcakes

Use a little less cake mixture when baking the cupcakes, so that when baked they don't quite reach the top of their cases. Spoon some glacé icing on top of the cooled cakes so that it floods out to the sides of the cases. Decorate with feathering, sprinkles, dragees, gold leaf or other decorations as desired.

Covering with sugarpaste

Covering cupcakes with sugarpaste works best if the baked cupcakes are flat – if they have peaked during baking, then trim to flatten. Next, simply roll out some sugarpaste in the desired colour, to a thickness of 5mm (¼in). Measure the top of the cupcakes, then cut out circles of sugarpaste to match. Spread a thin layer of buttercream over the cupcake, then secure the sugarpaste circle in place.

If you don't want to completely cover the tops with sugarpaste, cut out smaller shapes of the sugarpaste – hearts always look nice. Leave to dry completely on baking parchment. Position the sugarpaste shapes on buttercreamed cupcakes (the decorations should be stiff enough to stand up).

Mango and Passion Fruit Cupcakes

Hands-on time: 30 minutes
Cooking time: 25 minutes, plus cooling

4 ripe passion fruit

about 75ml (2½fl oz) orange juice

150g (5oz) unsalted butter, softened

250g (9oz) plain flour, sifted

175g (6oz) caster sugar

3 medium eggs

1 tbsp baking powder

75g (3oz) ready-to-eat dried mango, finely chopped

For the topping and decoration

100g (3½oz) cream cheese

25g (1oz) unsalted butter, softened

200g (7oz) icing sugar, sifted

1 large, ripe passion fruit

white sugar sprinkles

1 Preheat the oven to 180°C (160°C fan oven) mark 4. Line a 12–hole muffin tin with paper muffin cases.

2 Cut the passion fruit in half and pass the seeds and juice through a sieve into a jug. Discard the seeds. Top up with orange juice to make 150ml (¼ pint) liquid.

3 Put the butter, flour, caster sugar, eggs, baking powder and juice into a large bowl. Using a hand-held electric whisk, beat together, or beat with a wooden spoon, until pale and creamy. Add the chopped mango and fold in until combined. Spoon the mixture equally into the paper cases.

4 Bake for 25 minutes or until golden and risen. Leave to cool in the tin for 5 minutes, then transfer to a wire rack and leave to cool completely.

5 To make the topping, whisk together the cream cheese and butter until fluffy. Gradually add the icing sugar until combined. Cut the passion fruit in half and pass the seeds and juice through a sieve into the icing. Discard the seeds. Stir to combine, then, using a small palette knife, spread a little over the top of each cake. Scatter with the sugar sprinkles.

SAVE TIME

Store in an airtight container in the fridge. They will keep for two to three days.

Makes 12

Easter Cupcakes

Hands-on time: 30 minutes
Cooking time: 30 minutes, plus cooling and setting

2 medium eggs

75g (3oz) caster sugar

150ml (¼ pint) sunflower oil

150g (5oz) plain flour, sifted

½ tsp baking powder

1 tsp vanilla extract

15g (½oz) Rice Krispies

For the topping and decoration

100g (3½oz) white chocolate, broken into pieces

15g (½oz) unsalted butter

25g (1oz) Rice Krispies

12 chocolate mini eggs

1 Preheat the oven to 180°C (160°C fan oven) mark 4. Line a 6-hole muffin tin with paper muffin cases.

2 Separate the eggs, putting the whites in a clean, grease-free bowl and the egg yolks in another. Add the sugar to the yolks and, using a hand-held electric whisk, beat until pale and creamy, then whisk in the oil until combined.

3 Whisk the egg whites until soft peaks form. Using a metal spoon, quickly fold the flour, baking powder, vanilla extract and Rice Krispies into the egg yolk mixture until just combined. Add half the egg whites to the egg yolk mixture to loosen, then carefully fold in the remaining egg whites. Spoon the mixture equally into the paper cases.

4 Bake for 20–25 minutes until golden and risen. Leave to cool in the tin for 5 minutes, then transfer to a wire rack and leave to cool completely.

5 To make the topping, melt the chocolate and butter in a heatproof bowl over a pan of gently simmering water, making sure the base of the bowl doesn't touch the water. Heat gently until the chocolate has melted, stirring occasionally until smooth. Lift the bowl off the pan, add the Rice Krispies and fold in gently until coated. Spoon the mixture on top of each cake, pressing down lightly, then

top each with two chocolate eggs.
Stand the cupcakes on the wire rack
and leave for about 1 hour to set.

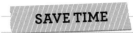

SAVE TIME

Store in an airtight container.
They will keep for three to five days.

Makes 6

Honeycomb Cream Cupcakes

Hands-on time: 30 minutes
Cooking time: 20 minutes, plus cooling

125g (4oz) unsalted butter, softened

50g (2oz) caster sugar

2 medium eggs

75g (3oz) clear honey

125g (4oz) self-raising flour, sifted

50g (2oz) rolled oats

½ tsp baking powder

1 tbsp milk

For the topping and decoration

125g (4oz) unsalted butter, softened

300g (11oz) golden icing sugar, sifted

2 tbsp milk

1 Crunchie bar, thinly sliced

1 Preheat the oven to 190°C (170°C fan oven) mark 5. Line a 12-hole muffin tin with nine paper muffin cases.

2 Using a hand-held electric whisk, beat the butter and caster sugar in a bowl, or beat with a wooden spoon, until pale and creamy. Gradually whisk in the eggs and honey until just combined. Using a metal spoon, fold in the flour, oats, baking powder and milk. Spoon the mixture equally into the paper cases.

3 Bake for 20 minutes or until the cupcakes are golden and risen. Cool in the tin for 5 minutes, then transfer to a wire rack and leave to cool completely.

4 To make the buttercream topping, put the butter into a bowl and whisk until fluffy. Gradually whisk in half the icing sugar, then add the milk and the remaining icing sugar and whisk until light and fluffy.

5 Insert a star nozzle into a piping bag, then fill the bag with the buttercream and pipe a swirl on the top of each cake. When ready to serve, decorate each with a few slices of Crunchie bar.

Cherry Bakewell Cupcakes

Hands-on time: 30 minutes, plus chilling
Cooking time: 25 minutes, plus cooling and setting

175g (6oz) unsalted butter, softened

175g (6oz) caster sugar

3 medium eggs

150g (5oz) self-raising flour, sifted

1 tsp baking powder

75g (3oz) ground almonds

1 tsp almond extract

75g (3oz) glacé cherries, finely chopped

For the topping and decoration

1 tbsp custard powder

100ml (3½fl oz) milk

50g (2oz) unsalted butter, softened

250g (9oz) icing sugar, sifted

red sugar sprinkles

SAVE TIME

Store in an airtight container in
the fridge. They will keep for two
to three days.

1 Preheat the oven to 190°C (170°C fan oven) mark 5. Line a 12-hole muffin tin with paper muffin cases.

2 Using a hand-held electric whisk, beat the butter and caster sugar in a bowl, or beat with a wooden spoon, until pale and creamy. Gradually whisk in the eggs until just combined. Using a metal spoon, fold in the flour, baking powder, ground almonds, almond extract and cherries until combined. Spoon the mixture equally into the paper cases.

3 Bake for 20 minutes or until golden and risen. Cool in the tin for 5 minutes, then transfer to a wire rack and leave to cool completely.

4 To make the topping, put the custard powder into a jug and add a little of the milk to make a smooth paste. Pour the remaining milk into a pan and bring just to the boil. Pour the hot milk on to the custard paste and stir. Return to the milk pan and heat gently for 1–2 minutes until it

thickens. Take off the heat, cover with dampened greaseproof paper to prevent a skin forming and leave to cool completely.

5 Put the custard into a bowl and, using a hand-held electric whisk, whisk in the butter. Chill for 30 minutes.

6 Gradually whisk the icing sugar into the chilled custard mixture until you have a smooth, thick icing. Using a small palette knife, spread a little custard cream over the top of each cake, then decorate with sugar sprinkles. Stand the cakes on the wire rack and leave for about 1 hour to set.

Makes 12

Mini Green Tea Cupcakes

Hands-on time: 40 minutes, plus infusing
Cooking time: 25 minutes, plus cooling

100ml (3½fl oz) milk

2 tsp loose green tea leaves

100g (3½oz) unsalted butter, softened

125g (4oz) caster sugar

2 medium eggs

150g (5oz) self-raising flour, sifted

½ tsp baking powder

For the topping and decoration

3 tsp loose green tea leaves

75g (3oz) unsalted butter, softened

250g (9oz) icing sugar, sifted

ready-made sugar flowers

1 Preheat the oven to 190°C (170°C fan oven) mark 5. Line a 12-hole muffin tin with paper muffin cases.

2 Put the milk into a small pan and bring to the boil. Add the green tea leaves and leave to infuse for 30 minutes.

3 Using a hand-held electric whisk, beat the butter and caster sugar in a bowl, or beat with a wooden spoon, until pale and creamy. Gradually whisk in the eggs until just combined. Pass the green tea milk through a sieve into the bowl, then discard the tea leaves. Using a metal spoon, fold in the flour and baking powder until combined. Spoon the mixture equally into the paper cases.

4 Bake for 18–20 minutes until golden and risen. Cool in the tin for 5 minutes, then transfer to a wire rack and leave to cool completely.

5 To make the topping, put the green tea leaves into a jug, add about 75ml (2½fl oz) boiling water and leave to infuse for 5 minutes.

6 Put the butter into a bowl and whisk until fluffy. Gradually add the icing sugar and whisk until combined. Pass the green tea through a sieve into the bowl, then discard the tea leaves. Continue to whisk until light and fluffy.

7 Insert a star nozzle into a piping bag, then fill the bag with the buttercream and pipe a swirl on the top of each cake. Decorate each with a sugar flower.

SAVE TIME

Store in an airtight container. They
will keep for three to five days.

Makes 12

Raspberry Ripple Cupcakes

Hands-on time: 30 minutes
Cooking time: 20 minutes, plus cooling

50g (2oz) seedless raspberry jam

50g (2oz) fresh raspberries

125g (4oz) unsalted butter, softened

100g (3½oz) caster sugar

2 medium eggs

1 tbsp milk

150g (5oz) self-raising flour, sifted

For the topping and decoration

150g (5oz) fresh raspberries

300ml (½ pint) whipping cream

50g (2oz) icing sugar, sifted

1 Preheat the oven to 190°C (170°C fan oven) mark 5. Line a 12-hole muffin tin with nine paper muffin cases.

2 Mix the raspberry jam with the 50g (2oz) raspberries, lightly crushing the raspberries. Put to one side.

3 Using a hand-held electric whisk, beat the butter and caster sugar in a bowl, or beat with a wooden spoon, until pale and creamy. Gradually whisk in the eggs and milk until just combined.

Using a metal spoon, fold in the flour until just combined, then carefully fold in the raspberry jam mixture until just marbled, being careful not to over-mix. Spoon the mixture equally into the paper cases.

4 Bake for 20 minutes or until golden and risen. Cool in the tin for 5 minutes, then transfer to a wire rack and leave to cool completely.

5 To make the decoration, reserve nine raspberries. Mash the remaining raspberries in a bowl with a fork. Pass through a sieve into a bowl to remove the seeds. Using a hand-held electric whisk, whip the cream and icing sugar together until stiff peaks form. Mix the raspberry purée into the cream until combined.

6 Insert a star nozzle into a piping bag, then fill the bag with the cream and pipe a swirl on the top of each cake. Decorate each with a raspberry.

SAVE TIME

Store in an airtight container in the fridge. They will keep for up to two days.

Makes 9

Pistachio and Polenta Cupcakes

Hands-on time: 35 minutes
Cooking time: 25 minutes, plus cooling

150g (5oz) shelled pistachio nuts

175g (6oz) unsalted butter, softened

175g (6oz) caster sugar

3 medium eggs

200g (7oz) fine polenta

½ tsp baking powder

150g (5oz) ground almonds

grated zest of 2 lemons

2 tbsp milk

For the icing

75g (3oz) unsalted butter, softened

300g (11oz) icing sugar, sifted

juice of 2 lemons

1 Preheat the oven to 180°C (160°C fan oven) mark 4. Line a 12-hole muffin tin with paper muffin cases.

2 Whiz the pistachio nuts in a food processor until really finely chopped.

3 Using a hand-held electric whisk, beat the butter and caster sugar in a bowl, or beat with a wooden spoon, until pale and creamy. Gradually whisk in the eggs until just combined. Using a metal spoon, fold in the polenta, baking powder, ground almonds, lemon zest, milk and 100g (3½oz) ground pistachio nuts until combined. Spoon the mixture equally into the paper cases.

4 Bake for 25 minutes or until golden and risen. Cool in the tin for 5 minutes, then transfer to a wire rack and leave to cool completely.

5 To make the icing, put the butter into a bowl and whisk until fluffy. Gradually whisk in half the icing sugar, then add the lemon juice and the remaining icing sugar, whisking until light and fluffy. Using a small palette knife, spread a little of the buttercream over the top of each cake, then sprinkle each with a little of the remaining chopped pistachio nuts.

Makes 12

Chocolate Fairy Cakes

Hands-on time: 20 minutes
Cooking time: about 15 minutes, plus cooling and setting

100g (3½oz) self-raising flour

25g (1oz) cocoa powder

1 tsp baking powder

125g (4oz) caster sugar

125g (4oz) unsalted butter, very soft

2 medium eggs

1 tbsp milk

50g (2oz) chocolate drops

For the icing and decoration

225g (8oz) icing sugar, sifted

assorted food colourings (optional)

sweets, sprinkles or coloured sugar

SAVE TIME

Store in an airtight container. They will keep for three to five days.

1 Preheat the oven to 200°C (180°C fan oven) mark 6. Put paper cases into 18 of the holes in two bun tins.

2 Sift the flour into a mixing bowl, then sift in the cocoa powder, baking powder and sugar. Add the butter, eggs and milk and beat with a hand-held electric whisk for 2 minutes or until the mixture is pale and very soft. Stir in the chocolate drops and spoon the mixture equally into the paper cases.

3 Bake for 10–15 minutes until risen and springy to the touch. Transfer to a wire rack and leave to cool completely.

4 To make the icing, put the icing sugar into a bowl and gradually blend in 2–3 tbsp warm water until the icing is fairly stiff, but spreadable. Add a couple of drops of food colouring, if you like.

5 Spread the tops of the cakes with the icing and decorate with sweets, sprinkles or coloured sugar, then leave to set.

Makes 18

Muffins and Mini Cakes

Cherry and Almond Muffins

Hands-on time: 10 minutes
Cooking time: 25 minutes, plus cooling

225g (8oz) plain flour

1 tsp baking powder

a pinch of salt

75g (3oz) caster sugar

50g (2oz) ground almonds

350g (12oz) glacé cherries,
roughly chopped

300ml (½ pint) milk

3 tbsp lemon juice

50ml (2fl oz) sunflower oil or melted
unsalted butter

1 large egg

1 tsp almond extract

roughly crushed sugar cubes to decorate

1 Preheat the oven to 190°C (170°C fan oven) mark 5. Line a 12-hole muffin tin with paper muffin cases.

2 Sift together the flour, baking powder and salt. Add the caster sugar and ground almonds. Stir in the chopped glacé cherries.

3 Whisk together the milk, lemon juice, oil or butter, the egg and almond extract. Pour into the dry ingredients and stir until all the ingredients are just combined – the mixture should be lumpy. Don't over-mix or the muffins will be tough.

4 Spoon the mixture equally into the paper cases and sprinkle with the crushed sugar cubes.

5 Bake for about 25 minutes until well risen and golden. Leave to cool in the tin for 5 minutes, then transfer to a wire rack and leave to cool completely. These muffins are best eaten on the day they are made.

Makes 12

Spiced Carrot Muffins

Hands-on time: 30 minutes
Cooking time: about 25 minutes, plus cooling

125g (4oz) unsalted butter, softened

125g (4oz) light muscovado sugar

3 pieces preserved stem ginger, drained and chopped

150g (5oz) self-raising flour, sifted

1½ tsp baking powder

1 tbsp ground mixed spice

25g (1oz) ground almonds

3 medium eggs

finely grated zest of ½ orange

150g (5oz) carrots, peeled and grated

50g (2oz) pecan nuts, chopped

50g (2oz) sultanas

3 tbsp white rum or orange liqueur (optional)

For the topping and decoration

200g (7oz) cream cheese

75g (3oz) icing sugar

1 tsp lemon juice

12 unsprayed rose petals (optional)

1 Preheat the oven to 180°C (160°C fan oven) mark 4. Line a 12-hole muffin tin with paper muffin cases.

2 Beat the butter, muscovado sugar and stem ginger together until pale and creamy. Add the flour, baking powder, spice, ground almonds, eggs and orange zest and beat well until combined. Stir in the carrots, pecan nuts and sultanas. Spoon the mixture equally into the paper cases.

3 Bake for 20–25 minutes until risen and just firm and a skewer inserted into the centre of a muffin comes out clean. Transfer to a wire rack and leave to cool completely.

4 To make the topping, beat the cream cheese in a bowl until softened. Beat in the icing sugar and lemon juice to give a smooth icing that just holds its shape.

5 Drizzle each muffin with a little liqueur, if you like. Using a small palette knife, spread a little icing over each muffin and decorate with a rose petal, if you like.

SAVE TIME

Store in an airtight container. They will keep for up to one week.

Makes 12

Blueberry Muffins

Hands-on time: 10 minutes
Cooking time: about 25 minutes, plus cooling

2 medium eggs
250ml (9fl oz) semi-skimmed milk
250g (9oz) golden granulated sugar
2 tsp vanilla extract
350g (12oz) plain flour
4 tsp baking powder
250g (9oz) blueberries, frozen
finely grated zest of 2 lemons

1 Preheat the oven to 200°C (180°C fan oven) mark 6. Line a 12-hole muffin tin with paper muffin cases.
2 Put the eggs, milk, sugar and vanilla extract into a bowl and mix well.
3 Sift the flour and baking powder together into another bowl, then add the blueberries and lemon zest. Toss together and make a well in the centre.
4 Pour the egg mixture into the flour and blueberries and mix in gently – over-beating will make the muffins tough. Spoon the mixture equally into the paper cases.
5 Bake for 20–25 minutes until risen and just firm. Transfer to a wire rack and leave to cool completely. These muffins are best eaten on the day they are made.

FREEZE AHEAD
Complete the recipe, then pack, seal and freeze the cold muffins. Thaw at cool room temperature to use.

Makes 12

Chocolate Banana Muffins

Hands-on time: 15 minutes
Cooking time: 20 minutes, plus cooling

275g (10oz) self-raising flour

1 tsp bicarbonate of soda

½ tsp salt

3 large bananas, about 450g (1lb)

125g (4oz) golden caster sugar

1 large egg, beaten

50ml (2fl oz) semi-skimmed milk

75g (3oz) unsalted butter, melted
   and cooled

50g (2oz) plain chocolate, chopped

1 Preheat the oven to 180°C (160°C fan oven) mark 4. Line a 12-hole muffin tin with paper muffin cases. Sift the flour, bicarbonate of soda and salt into a large mixing bowl and put to one side.

2 Peel the bananas and mash with a fork in a bowl. Add the sugar, egg, milk and melted and cooled butter and mix until well combined.

3 Add this to the flour mixture, with the chopped chocolate. Stir gently, using only a few strokes, until the flour is only just incorporated – do not over-mix. The mixture should be lumpy. Spoon the mixture equally into the paper cases, half-filling them.

4 Bake for 20 minutes or until the muffins are well risen and golden. Transfer to a wire rack and leave to cool. Serve warm or cold. These muffins are best eaten on the day they are made.

FREEZE AHEAD

Complete the recipe, then pack, seal and freeze the cold muffins. Thaw at cool room temperature to use.

Makes 12

Double Chocolate Muffins

Hands-on time: 20 minutes
Cooking time: about 25 minutes, plus cooling

125g (4oz) unsalted butter

100g (3½oz) plain chocolate, chopped

225g (8oz) plain flour

1 tsp bicarbonate of soda

40g (1½oz) cocoa powder, sifted

175g (6oz) golden caster sugar

200g (7oz) white chocolate, chopped

a pinch of salt

1 medium egg

200ml (7fl oz) milk

150g carton natural yogurt

1 tsp vanilla extract

1 Preheat the oven to 190°C (170°C fan oven) mark 5. Line a 12-hole muffin tin with paper muffin cases.

2 Melt the butter and plain chocolate in a heatproof bowl over a pan of gently simmering water, making sure the base of the bowl doesn't touch the water. Mix together very gently and leave to cool a little.

3 Meanwhile, put the flour into a large bowl. Add the bicarbonate of soda, cocoa powder, sugar, white chocolate and salt and stir everything together. Put the egg, milk, yogurt and vanilla extract into a jug and beat together.

4 Pour both the egg mixture and the chocolate mixture on to the dry ingredients, then roughly fold together. Be careful not to over-mix, or the muffins won't rise properly. Spoon the mixture equally into the paper cases.

5 Bake for 20–25 minutes until well risen and springy. Transfer to a wire rack and leave to cool before serving.

SAVE TIME

Store in an airtight container. They will keep for up to three days.

Makes 12

Brown Sugar Muffins

Hands-on time: 10 minutes
Cooking time: about 35 minutes, plus cooling

12 brown sugar cubes
150g (5oz) plain flour
1½ tsp baking powder
¼ tsp salt
1 medium egg, beaten
40g (1½oz) golden caster sugar
50g (2oz) unsalted butter, melted
½ tsp vanilla extract
100ml (3½fl oz) milk

1 Preheat the oven to 200°C (180°C fan oven) mark 6. Line a 6-hole muffin tin with paper muffin cases.
2 Roughly crush the sugar cubes and put to one side. Sift together the flour, baking powder and salt.
3 Put the beaten egg, caster sugar, melted butter, vanilla extract and milk into a large bowl and stir to combine.
4 Fold in the sifted flour and spoon the mixture equally into the paper cases. Sprinkle with the brown sugar.
5 Bake for 30–35 minutes until well risen and springy. Transfer to a wire rack and leave to cool before serving. These muffins are best eaten on the day they are made.

FREEZE AHEAD
Complete the recipe, then pack, seal and freeze the cold muffins. Thaw at cool room temperature to use.

Makes 6

Bran and Apple Muffins

Hands-on time: 20 minutes
Cooking time: 30 minutes, plus cooling

250ml (9fl oz) semi-skimmed milk

2 tbsp orange juice

50g (2oz) All Bran

9 ready-to-eat dried prunes

100g (3½oz) light muscovado sugar

2 medium egg whites

1 tbsp golden syrup

150g (5oz) plain flour, sifted

1 tsp baking powder

1 tsp ground cinnamon

1 eating apple, peeled and grated

demerara sugar to sprinkle

1 Preheat the oven to 190°C (170°C fan oven) mark 5. Line a 10-hole muffin tin with paper muffin cases.

2 Put the milk, orange juice and All Bran into a bowl and stir to mix. Put to one side for 10 minutes.

3 Put the prunes into a food processor or blender with 100ml (3½fl oz) water and whiz for 2–3 minutes to make a purée, then add the muscovado sugar and whiz briefly to mix.

4 Put the egg whites into a large, grease-free bowl and, using a hand-held electric whisk, beat until soft peaks form. Add the whites to the milk mixture with the golden syrup, flour, baking powder, cinnamon, grated apple and prune mixture. Fold all the ingredients together gently – don't over-mix. Spoon the mixture equally into the paper cases.

5 Bake for 30 minutes or until well risen and golden brown. Transfer to a wire rack and leave to cool completely. Sprinkle with demerara sugar just before serving. These muffins are best eaten on the day they are made.

Makes 10

Banana and Pecan Muffins

Hands-on time: 10 minutes
Cooking time: 20 minutes, plus cooling

275g (10oz) self-raising flour

1 tsp bicarbonate of soda

pinch of salt

3 very ripe large bananas, about
    450g (1lb), peeled and mashed

125g (4oz) golden caster sugar

1 large egg

50ml (2fl oz) milk

75g (3oz) unsalted butter, melted

50g (2oz) chopped roasted pecan nuts

1 Preheat the oven to 180°C (160°C fan oven) mark 4. Line a 12-hole muffin tin with paper muffin cases.
2 Sift together the flour, bicarbonate of soda and salt and put to one side.
3 Combine the bananas, sugar, egg and milk, then pour in the melted butter and mix well. Add to the flour mixture with the nuts, stirring quickly and gently with just a few strokes. Half-fill the muffin cases.
4 Bake for 20 minutes or until golden and risen. Transfer to a wire rack and leave to cool.

SAVE TIME

The secret to really light, fluffy muffins is a light hand, so be sure to sift the flour. Stir the mixture as little as possible; it's okay if it looks a little lumpy. Over-mixing will give tough, chewy results.

Makes 12

Chocolate Whoopie Pies

Hands-on time: 30 minutes
Cooking time: about 12 minutes, plus cooling

1 large egg

150g (5oz) caster sugar

75g (3oz) butter, melted

150g (5oz) crème fraîche

1 tsp vanilla extract

1½–2 tbsp milk

200g (7oz) plain flour

75g (3oz) cocoa powder

½ tsp bicarbonate of soda

For the filling

115g (3¾oz) unsalted butter, softened

200g (7oz) icing sugar, sifted

1 tsp vanilla extract

milk (optional)

1 Preheat the oven to 180°C (160°C fan oven) mark 4. Line two large baking sheets with baking parchment.

2 Whisk the egg and caster sugar together until thick and light in colour. Beat in the melted butter, crème fraîche, vanilla extract and milk.

3 Sift together the flour, cocoa powder and bicarbonate of soda. Beat into the egg mixture until smooth – it will make a very thick mixture but you should be able to pipe it. Add a drop more milk if necessary.

4 Insert a large nozzle into a piping bag, then fill the bag with the mixture and pipe walnut-sized balls on the baking sheets, spacing them well apart.

5 Bake for 10–12 minutes until golden and risen. Cool on the baking sheet for 1–2 minutes until firm, then transfer to a wire rack and leave to cool completely.

6 To make the buttercream filling, cream together the butter and icing sugar until fluffy. Beat in the vanilla extract. Beat in a little milk, if necessary, to make the icing a spreadable consistency. Sandwich the whoopie halves together with the buttercream.

Celebration Cakes

Take 5 Icing Recipes

Glacé Icing

To make 225g (8oz), enough to cover
18 fairy cakes, you will need:
225g (8oz) icing sugar, a few drops
of vanilla or almond flavouring
(optional), food colouring (optional).

1 Sift the icing sugar into a bowl.
   Add a few drops of flavouring, if
   you like.
2 Using a wooden spoon, gradually
   stir in 2-3 tbsp boiling water until
   the mixture is the consistency
   of thick cream. Beat until white
   and smooth and the icing is thick
   enough to coat the back of the
   spoon. Add colouring, if you like,
   and use immediately.

Royal Icing

Royal icing can also be bought in packs from supermarkets. Simply add water or egg white to use. To make 450g (1lb), enough to cover the top and sides of a 20.5cm (8in) cake, you will need:

2 medium egg whites, ¼ tsp lemon juice, 450g (1lb) icing sugar, sifted, 1 tsp glycerine.

1 Put the egg whites and lemon juice into a clean bowl and stir to break up the egg whites. Add sufficient icing sugar to mix to the consistency of un-whipped cream. Continue mixing and adding small quantities of icing sugar until the desired consistency is reached, mixing well and gently beating after each addition. The icing should be smooth, glossy and light, almost like a cold meringue in texture, but not aerated. Do not add the icing sugar too quickly or it will produce a dull heavy icing. Stir in the glycerine until well blended. (Alternatively, for large quantities of royal icing, use a food mixer on the lowest speed, following the same instructions as before.)

2 Allow the icing to settle before using it; cover the surface with a piece of damp clingfilm and seal well, excluding all the air.

3 Stir the icing thoroughly before use to disperse any air bubbles, then, if necessary, adjust the consistency by adding more sifted icing sugar.

Apricot Glaze

To make 450g (1lb), you will need:
450g (1lb) apricot jam.

1   Put the jam and 2 tbsp water into
    a pan and heat gently, stirring
    occasionally, until the jam has
    dissolved. Boil the jam rapidly
    for 1 minute, then strain through
    a sieve.
2   Using a wooden spoon, rub
    through as much fruit as possible.
    Discard the skins left in the sieve.
3   Pour the glaze into a clean, hot jar,
    then seal with a clean lid and leave
    to cool. Store in the fridge for up
    to two months. You only need
    3–4 tbsp apricot glaze for a 23cm
    (9in) cake, so this quantity will
    glaze 6–7 cakes.

Almond Paste

To make 450g (1lb) almond paste,
enough to cover the top and sides
of an 18cm (7in) round cake or 15cm
(6in) square cake, you will need:
225g (8oz) ground almonds, 125g
(4oz) golden caster sugar, 125g (4oz)
sifted golden icing sugar, 1 large
egg, 2 tsp lemon juice, 1 tsp sherry,
1–2 drops vanilla extract.

1   Put the ground almonds and
    sugars into a bowl and stir
    to combine. In another bowl,
    whisk together the remaining
    ingredients, then add to the dry
    ingredients.
2   Stir well to mix, pounding gently
    to release some of the oil from the
    almonds. Knead with your hands
    until smooth, then cover until
    ready to use.

SAVE TIME

If you wish to avoid using raw egg
to bind the almond paste, mix the
other liquid ingredients with a little
water instead.

Fondant (Sugarpaste) Icing

To make 500g (1lb 2oz), enough to cover the top and sides of an 18cm (7in) round cake or 15cm (6in) square cake, you will need:

500g (1lb 2oz) golden icing sugar, plus extra to dust, 1 medium egg white, 2 tbsp liquid glucose, warmed, 1 tsp vanilla extract.

1. Whiz the icing sugar in a food processor for 30 seconds, then add the egg white, glucose and vanilla extract and whiz for 2–3 minutes until the mixture forms a ball.
2. Wrap completely in clingfilm and store in a polythene bag with all the air excluded.

Chocolate Birthday Cake

Egg Free

🍴 **Hands-on time:** 30 minutes, plus cooling
Cooking time: about 1¼ hours, plus cooling

150ml (¼ pint) sunflower oil, plus extra to grease

75g (3oz) creamed coconut

25g (1oz) plain chocolate, broken into pieces

50g (2oz) cocoa powder

350g (12oz) self-raising flour

1 tsp baking powder

a pinch of salt

175g (6oz) light muscovado sugar

For the icing

350g (12oz) plain chocolate, broken into small pieces

150ml (¼ pint) double cream

white and milk chocolate Maltesers to decorate

1 Grease a 1.7 litre (3 pint), 30.5 × 10cm (12 × 4in) loaf tin and line with greaseproof paper. Put the coconut into a heatproof bowl, pour on 425ml (14½fl oz) boiling water and stir to dissolve. Leave to cool for 30 minutes.

2 Melt the chocolate in a heatproof bowl set over a pan of gently simmering water, making sure the base of the bowl doesn't touch the water. Stir until smooth, then remove the bowl from the pan and leave to cool slightly. Preheat the oven to 180°C (160°C fan oven) mark 4.

3 Sift the cocoa powder, flour, baking powder and salt into a bowl. Stir in the sugar and make a well in the middle. Add the coconut mixture, melted chocolate and oil and beat to make a smooth batter. Pour the cake batter into the prepared tin.

4 Bake for 1–1¼ hours or until risen and just firm to the touch (if necessary, after about 40 minutes, cover the top of the cake loosely with foil if it appears to be browning too quickly). Leave in the tin for 10 minutes, then turn out on to a wire rack (leave the lining paper on) and leave to cool completely. When the cake is cold,

peel off the lining paper and trim to neaten the edges.

5 To make the icing, put the chocolate into a heatproof bowl. Heat the cream to just below boiling point, then pour on to the chocolate and stir until melted. Leave to cool, beating occasionally, until thick – pop it into the fridge for 30 minutes to help thicken, if necessary.

6 Cut the cold cake in half horizontally and spread about one-third of the icing over the bottom half, then sandwich the layers together.

Spread the rest of the icing evenly over the top and sides of the cake. Decorate the top of the cake with alternate rows of milk and white Maltesers. Lay an edging of alternate milk and white Maltesers around the bottom of the cake to decorate.

Cuts into 12 slices

Take 5 Frosting Recipes

Vanilla Frosting

To make about 175g (6oz), enough to cover the top and sides of an 18cm (7in) cake, you will need:
150g (5oz) icing sugar, 5 tsp vegetable oil, 1 tbsp milk, a few drops of vanilla extract.

1 Sift the icing sugar into a bowl and, using a wooden spoon, beat in the oil, milk and vanilla extract until smooth.
2 Use the icing immediately, spreading it over the cake with a wet palette knife.

Coffee Fudge Frosting

To make 400g (14oz), enough to cover the top and sides of a 20.5cm (8in) cake, you will need:
50g (2oz) unsalted butter, 125g (4oz) light muscovado sugar, 2 tbsp single cream or milk, 1 tbsp coffee granules, 200g (7oz) golden icing sugar, sifted.

1 Put the butter, muscovado sugar and cream or milk into a pan. Dissolve the coffee in 2 tbsp boiling water and add to the pan. Heat gently until the sugar dissolves, then bring to the boil and boil briskly for 3 minutes.
2 Take off the heat and gradually stir in the icing sugar. Beat well with a wooden spoon for 1 minute until smooth.
3 Use the frosting immediately, spreading it over the cake with a wet palette knife, or dilute with a little water to use as a smooth coating.

Chocolate Fudge Frosting

Omit the coffee. Add 75g (3oz) plain chocolate, in pieces, to the pan with the butter at the beginning of step 1.

American Frosting

To make 225g (8oz), enough to cover the top and sides of a 20.5cm (8in) cake, you will need:
1 large egg white, 225g (8oz) golden caster or granulated sugar, a pinch of cream of tartar.

1 Whisk the egg white in a clean, grease-free bowl until stiff. Put the sugar, 4 tbsp water and the cream of tartar into a heavy-based pan. Heat gently, stirring, until the sugar has dissolved. Bring to the boil, without stirring, and boil until the sugar syrup registers 115°C on a sugar thermometer.
2 Remove from the heat and, as soon as the bubbles subside, pour the syrup on to the egg white in a thin stream, whisking constantly until thick and white. Leave to cool slightly.
3 When the frosting begins to turn dull around the edges and is almost cold, pour quickly over the cake and spread evenly with a palette knife.

Seven-minute Frosting

To make about 175g (6oz), enough to cover the top and sides of an 18cm (7in) cake, you will need:
1 medium egg white, 175g (6oz) caster sugar, a pinch of salt, a pinch of cream of tartar.

1 Put all the ingredients including 2 tbsp water into a heatproof bowl and whisk lightly using an electric or hand whisk.
2 Put the bowl over a pan of hot water, making sure the base of the bowl doesn't touch the water, and heat, whisking continuously, until the mixture thickens sufficiently to stand in peaks – this should take about 7 minutes.
3 Pour the frosting over the top of the cake and spread with a palette knife.

Black Forest Birthday Gateau

Hands-on time: 30 minutes
Cooking time: about 50 minutes, plus cooling

125g (4oz) unsalted butter, melted and
 left to cool for 10 minutes

200g (7oz) plain flour

50g (2oz) cornflour

50g (2oz) cocoa powder, plus extra
 to dust

2 tsp espresso instant coffee powder

1 tsp baking powder

4 large eggs, separated

300g (11oz) golden caster sugar

2 × 300g jars morello cherries in syrup

2 tbsp Kirsch

200ml (7fl oz) double cream

2 tbsp icing sugar, sifted

For the decoration

fresh cherries

chocolate curls

1 Preheat the oven to 180°C (160°C
 fan oven) mark 4. Brush a little of
 the melted butter over the base and
 sides of a 20.5 × 9cm (8 × 3½in) round
 cake tin. Line the base and sides with
 baking parchment.

2 Sift the flour, cornflour, cocoa
 powder, coffee powder and baking
 powder together three times – this
 helps to add air and makes sure the
 ingredients are well mixed.

3 Put the egg yolks, caster sugar and
 100ml (3½fl oz) cold water into a
 freestanding mixer and whisk for
 8 minutes or until the mixture leaves
 a trail for 3 seconds when the whisk
 is lifted.

4 Add the rest of the melted butter,
 pouring it around the edge of the bowl
 so that the mixture doesn't lose any
 air, then quickly fold it in, followed by
 the sifted flour mixture in two batches.

5 In another grease-free bowl, whisk the
 egg whites until stiff peaks form, then
 fold a spoonful into the cake mixture
 to loosen. Carefully fold in the rest of
 the egg whites, making sure that there
 are no white blobs left. Pour into the
 prepared tin.

6 Bake for 45–50 minutes until a skewer
 inserted into the centre comes out

clean. Leave in the tin for 10 minutes, then turn out on to a wire rack (leave the lining paper on) and leave to cool completely.

7 When the cake is cold, peel off the lining paper and trim the top to make a flat surface. Turn the cake over so that the top becomes the base. Using a long serrated bread knife, carefully cut horizontally into three. Drain the cherries, reserving 250ml (9fl oz) of the syrup. Pour the syrup into a pan and simmer to reduce by half. Stir in the Kirsch. Brush the hot syrup on each layer of the cake – including the top – using up all the liquid.

8 Lightly whip the cream with the icing sugar. Spread one-third over the bottom layer of the cake and cover with half the cherries. Top with the next cake layer and repeat with another third of the cream and the remaining cherries. Top with the final cake layer and spread the remaining cream over it. Decorate with fresh cherries, chocolate curls and a dusting of cocoa powder.

Cuts into 12 slices

Split It

Some recipes require cakes to be split into two or three layers before being sandwiched back together with a filling.

Splitting cakes with a knife

If you want a level top to your cake, then it is worth turning the cake upside down before splitting. Alternatively, if the cake has risen at the top, you can trim it level using a knife.

1   Leave the cake to cool completely before splitting, then place on a board or a turntable.

2   Using a large knife or large serrated knife with a shallow thin blade (such as a bread knife), mark the number of layers required on the side of the cake. Next, cut a small notch from the top to the bottom on one side of the cake so that you will know where to line the layers up. Alternatively, put two cocktail sticks above each other, one in the top half, one in the lower half.

3   Using a sawing motion, cut midway between the top and bottom of the cake – or where needed to make your first layer. Turn the cake slowly while cutting, taking care to keep the blade parallel with the base, until you have cut all the way around the sides.

Splitting cakes with a cake-cutting wire

These easy-to-use cake wires are available from most specialist cake shops or via websites. They have a height-adjustable fine serrated blade, supported by a handle and stabilising feet to ensure regular cutting. Using gentle sawing motions, you can cleanly and neatly cut a cake into multiple layers. The only constriction is the width of the tool, so make sure you buy one wider than your cake.

4   Cut through the central core and lift off the top of the cake. If your cake is delicate, you might want to slide a non-lipped cake base between the layers to support the top of the cake as you lift it off. Cut more layers as needed.

Fill It

Fillings come in different textures, consistencies, flavours and colours. A filling is the essential part of assembling a layered cake or gateau, as it offers moisture, flavour and a way of sandwiching the layers back together to give the cake a good shape.

Filling cakes with icing or frosting

Some fillings team better with some cakes than others – if a cake is light and delicate in texture, it needs to be filled with a light cream filling or frosting, while a more substantial cake will tolerate a richer type of filling. A light cake will not support a heavy filling, which can cause the cake to collapse and fall apart on slicing.

To fill a cake

Put the cake on a board and decide on the filling. Once decided, you need to get the consistency right. If the filling is too firm, it will pull the crumbs off the cake as you spread it or even rip it. If too soft, it will ooze out of the cake once it is sandwiched back together.

First dollop some of the filling in the middle of the cake, then spread with a metal knife (a palette knife is good, if you have one) that has been dipped briefly into a jug of hot water. Re-dip the knife as needed to obtain a smooth, level finish. Alternatively, pipe fillings such as buttercream or whipped cream to create an even finish.

Filling options include whipped (flavoured) cream, flavoured frostings, buttercreams, fudge icings and jams, which team well with cream, frosting and icings.

To rebuild a cake

Once you have covered the base layer of your cake with filling, carefully position on the next layer of cake, using your cut notch or cocktail sticks to guide you. Repeat the filling and layering process as needed.

Buttercream

To cover the top and sides of a 20.5cm (8in) cake, you will need: 75g (3oz) unsalted butter, 175g (6oz) icing sugar, sifted, a few drops of vanilla extract, 1–2 tbsp milk.

1 Soften the butter in a mixing bowl, then beat until light and fluffy.
2 Gradually stir in the remaining ingredients and beat until smooth. Either use immediately or cover with clingfilm to exclude air.

Variations

· Replace the vanilla with a little grated orange, lemon or lime zest, and use some of the fruit's juice in place of the milk.
· Blend 1 tbsp cocoa powder with 2 tbsp boiling water. Cool, then add to the mixture in place of the milk.
· For a strong colour, use food colouring paste; liquid colouring gives a paler effect.

Toasted Hazelnut Meringue Cake

Hands-on time: 10 minutes
Cooking time: 30 minutes, plus cooling

oil to grease

175g (6oz) skinned hazelnuts, toasted

3 large egg whites

175g (6oz) golden caster sugar

250g tub mascarpone cheese

285ml (9½fl oz) double cream

3 tbsp Bailey's Irish Cream liqueur

140g (4½oz) frozen raspberries

340g jar redcurrant jelly

FREEZE AHEAD

Freezing the meringue makes it slightly softer but no less tasty. Complete the recipe, but don't put on a serving plate or drizzle with liqueur. Using the paper, lift the cake into the freezer and freeze until solid. Once solid, store in a sturdy container in the freezer for up to one month. Thaw overnight in the fridge, then complete the recipe.

1 Preheat the oven to 190°C (170°C fan oven) mark 5. Lightly oil two 18cm (7in) sandwich tins and base-line with baking parchment. Whiz the hazelnuts in a food processor until finely chopped.

2 Put the egg whites into a large, grease-free bowl and whisk until stiff peaks form. Whisk in the sugar, a spoonful at a time. Using a metal spoon, fold in half the nuts. Divide the mixture equally between the tins and spread evenly.

3 Bake both cakes on the middle shelf of the oven for about 30 minutes, then leave to cool in the tins for 30 minutes.

4 To make the filling, put the mascarpone cheese into a bowl. Beat in the cream and liqueur until smooth. Put the raspberries and redcurrant jelly into a pan and heat gently until the jelly has dissolved. Sieve, then leave to cool.

5 Use a palette knife to loosen the edges of the meringues, then turn out on to a wire rack and peel off the lining paper. Put a large sheet of baking parchment on a board and sit one meringue on top, flat-side down. Spread one-third of the mascarpone mixture over the meringue. Top with the other meringue, then cover the whole cake with the rest of the mascarpone mixture, then drizzle with the raspberry purée. Sprinkle with the remaining hazelnuts. Carefully put the cake on a serving plate and drizzle with more liqueur, if you like.

Cuts into 8 slices

Easter Chocolate Fudge Cake

Hands-on time: 30 minutes
Cooking time: about 50 minutes, plus cooling

175g (6oz) unsalted butter, softened, plus extra to grease

150g (5oz) plain flour

50g (2oz) cocoa powder

1 tsp baking powder

a pinch of salt

150g (5oz) light muscovado sugar

3 medium eggs, beaten

250ml (9fl oz) soured cream

1 tsp vanilla extract

For the icing and decoration

100g (3½oz) plain chocolate, finely chopped

150g (5oz) unsalted butter, softened

125g (4oz) cream cheese

175g (6oz) icing sugar, sifted

50g (2oz) chocolate curls, lightly crushed

foil-covered chocolate eggs

1 Preheat the oven to 180°C (160°C fan oven) mark 4. Grease a 20.5cm (8in) springform tin and line with greaseproof paper, then grease the paper lightly.

2 Sift the flour, cocoa powder, baking powder and salt into a large bowl. Using an electric mixer or electric beaters, mix the butter and muscovado sugar in a separate bowl until pale and fluffy – this should take about 5 minutes. Gradually add the beaten eggs, mixing well after each addition. Add a little of the flour mixture if the butter mixture looks like curdling. In one go, add the remaining flour mixture, the soured cream and vanilla extract, then fold in everything gently with a metal spoon. Spoon into the prepared tin.

3 Bake for 40–50 minutes until a skewer inserted into the centre comes out clean. Leave to cool in the tin.

4 To make the icing, melt the chocolate in a heatproof bowl set over a pan of gently simmering water, making sure the base of the bowl doesn't touch the water. Leave to cool for 15 minutes. In a separate bowl, beat the butter and cream cheese with a wooden spoon

until combined. Beat in the icing sugar, then the cooled chocolate. Take care not to over-beat the mixture – it should be fudgey, not stiff.

5 When the cake is cold, turn it out of the tin and peel off the lining paper.

Cut in half horizontally and use some icing to sandwich the layers together. Transfer to a cake stand, then ice the top and sides, smoothing with a palette knife. Decorate with crushed chocolate curls and chocolate eggs.

Cuts into 12 slices

Simnel Cake

Hands-on time: 30 minutes
Cooking time: about 1 hour 25 minutes, plus cooling

225g (8oz) butter, softened, plus extra
  to grease

225g (8oz) self-raising flour

2 tsp ground mixed spice

400g (14oz) mixed dried fruit

150g (5oz) light muscovado sugar

50g (2oz) golden syrup

finely grated zest of 2 lemons

4 medium eggs, lightly beaten

For the decoration

icing sugar to dust

500g (1lb 2oz) marzipan

2 tbsp apricot jam

length of yellow ribbon

1 Preheat the oven to 170°C (150°C fan oven) mark 3. Grease a 20.5cm (8in) round cake tin and line with baking parchment.

2 Put the flour, mixed spice and dried fruit into a large bowl and stir together until combined. Put the butter, muscovado sugar, golden syrup and lemon zest into a separate large bowl

and, using a hand-held electric whisk, beat together until pale and fluffy – this should take about 3 minutes. Gradually beat in the eggs, whisking well after each addition. Add the flour mixture and fold everything together with a large metal spoon. Pour the mixture into the prepared tin.

3 Bake for 1 hour, then cover the top of the cake with foil and bake for a further 25 minutes or until the cake is risen and springy to the touch. A skewer inserted into the centre should come out clean, but don't be tempted to test too early or the cake may sink. Leave the cake to cool completely in the tin. When the cake is cold, turn it out of the tin, peel off the lining paper and transfer to a serving plate.

4 To decorate, dust the worksurface with icing sugar and roll out two-thirds of the marzipan until large enough for a 20.5cm (8in) circle (cut around the base of the cake tin). Heat the jam with 1 tsp water in a small pan over

a medium heat until runny. Brush the top of the cake with some jam, then lay the marzipan circle on top and gently press down to stick it to the cake. Using a small knife, score lines on top of the cake to make a diamond pattern. Crimp the edge of the marzipan using the thumb and forefinger of one hand and the index finger of the other.

5 Roll the remaining marzipan into 11 equal-sized balls. Brush the underside of each with a little jam or water and stick to the top of the cake. If you like, use a blowtorch to lightly brown the marzipan. To finish, secure a yellow ribbon around the cake. Serve in slices.

Cuts into 12 slices

Cheat's Chocolate Cake

Hands-on time: 10 minutes
Cooking time: about 40 minutes, plus cooling

oil to grease

400g (14oz) chocolate hazelnut spread

3 medium eggs

125g (4oz) self-raising flour

200g carton full-fat cream cheese

chocolate mini eggs to decorate
 (optional)

1 Preheat the oven to 180°C (160° fan oven) mark 4. Grease a 20.5cm (8in) round cake tin and line with baking parchment.

2 Put 300g (11oz) of the chocolate hazelnut spread, the eggs and flour into a large bowl and mix until combined. Spoon the mixture into the prepared tin and level the surface.

3 Bake for 35–40 minutes until a skewer inserted into the centre comes out clean. Leave to cool in the tin for 10 minutes, then turn out on to a wire rack (leave the lining paper on) and leave to cool completely. When the cake is cold, peel off the lining paper.

4 To make the icing, mix the cream cheese with the remaining chocolate hazelnut spread until well combined. Spread the icing on top of the cake and decorate with chocolate mini eggs, if you like. Serve in slices.

White Chocolate Cappuccino Cake

Hands-on time: 45 minutes
Cooking time: about 50 minutes, plus cooling

300g (11oz) unsalted butter, at room
temperature, plus extra to grease

250g (9oz) self-raising flour, plus extra
to dust

200g (7oz) caster sugar

3 large eggs, at room temperature,
beaten

1½ tsp baking powder

50ml (2fl oz) milk

1 tsp vanilla extract

125g (4oz) white chocolate

125ml (4fl oz) double cream

1½–2 tbsp espresso coffee, cooled

75g (3oz) icing sugar, sifted, plus extra
to dust

50g (2oz) plain chocolate, grated

40g (1½oz) hazelnuts, roasted
and chopped

fresh small roses to decorate

1 Preheat the oven to 180°C (160°C
fan oven) mark 4. Grease a deep,
non-stick 20.5cm (8in) cake tin and
dust with flour.

2 Beat together the caster sugar and 175g
(6oz) butter until pale and creamy.
Gradually add the eggs, beating well
after each addition. Add 1 tbsp flour
if the mixture looks like curdling.
Fold in the remaining flour and the
baking powder, followed by the milk
and vanilla extract. Spoon into the
prepared tin and level the surface.

3 Bake for 40–50 minutes until a skewer
inserted into the centre comes out
clean. Leave to cool in the tin for
5 minutes, then turn out on to a wire
rack and leave to cool completely.

4 Cut the cake in half horizontally.
Grate 25g (1oz) white chocolate, then
beat together with the cream and
coffee until the mixture holds its
shape. Use to sandwich the two
cake halves together.

5 Chop the remaining white chocolate
and melt in a bowl set over a pan
of gently simmering water, making
sure the base of the bowl doesn't

touch the water. Leave to cool for 10 minutes. Beat together the remaining butter and the icing sugar until pale and creamy. Beat in the cooled white chocolate, then spread over the sides and top of the cake.

6 Mix the plain chocolate with the nuts and press around the side of the cake. Decorate with small roses dusted with icing sugar.

SAVE TIME

Complete the recipe to the end of step 2 up to 24 hours ahead. Return to the tin when cool and wrap in clingfilm. Complete the recipe to serve.

Cuts into 10 slices

Sleeping Beauty's Castle

Hands-on time: 1 hour

1 × white ready-iced 23cm (9in) square
   sponge cake

5 raspberry or strawberry Swiss rolls,
   about 9cm (3½in) long

450g (1lb) white sugarpaste

icing sugar to dust

Apricot Glaze (see page 134)

1 × white ready-iced 15cm (6in) round
   sponge cake

2 × quantities of pink buttercream icing
   (see page 145)

5 ice cream sugar cones

For the decoration

multicoloured sprinkles

red, pink, yellow, green and white
   writing icing

sugar flowers

small round pink sweets or pink
   edible balls

paper flag

1 Put the square cake on a 30.5cm (12in) square cake board. Measure the circumference of a Swiss roll with a piece of string. Divide the sugarpaste into five pieces. Lightly dust a worksurface with icing sugar, then roll out each piece of sugarpaste thinly into a rectangle the length of the Swiss roll by the length of the piece of string. Neaten the edges with a sharp knife. Brush each piece of icing with apricot glaze and roll around a Swiss roll, gently working the edges together to seal.

2 Put the round cake in the centre of the square cake. Put a dollop of buttercream at each corner of the square cake and position four of the Swiss rolls, with the sealed edge facing inwards, to make towers. Smooth pink buttercream over four of the cones and spread a little on top of each tower. Dip the tips of the cones in sprinkles, then fix on top of the towers. Using red writing icing, draw a simple

window, divided by four panes, at the top of each tower.

3 At the front of the castle, use red writing icing to draw a door with a doorknob. Use pink and yellow writing icing to draw small flowers around the castle and below the windows. Fix a few sugar flowers to the walls with writing icing. Connect the flowers with green writing icing to represent stems. Use the green writing icing to draw clumps of grass around the base of the wall. Stick a sugar flower to the paper flag with writing icing.

4 Position the remaining Swiss roll in the centre of the round cake. Cover the remaining cone with buttercream, dip in sprinkles and position on top of the round cake, fixing with a little buttercream. Draw on windows and decorate with sugar flowers as before. Make blobs of white writing icing, just touching each other, around the edges of the cones and decorate with pink sweets or edible balls. Stick the paper flag into the central tower.

Cuts into 35 small slices

Red Velvet Cake

Hands-on time: 20 minutes
Cooking time: about 1 hour 10 minutes, plus cooling

200g (7oz) unsalted butter, softened, plus extra to grease

250g (9oz) plain flour

40g (1½oz) cocoa powder

1½ tsp baking powder

225g (8oz) caster sugar

2 large eggs, beaten

250ml (9fl oz) soured cream

1 tbsp white wine vinegar

1 tsp bicarbonate of soda

¼ tsp red food colouring paste

For the frosting

400g (14oz) cream cheese

125g (4oz) unsalted butter, softened

125g (4oz) icing sugar

red sugar sprinkles to decorate (optional)

1 Preheat the oven to 180°C (160°C fan oven) mark 4. Grease a deep 20.5cm (8in) cake tin and line with baking parchment.

2 Sift the flour, cocoa powder and baking powder into a medium bowl. In a separate large bowl and using a hand-held electric whisk, beat together the butter and caster sugar until pale and fluffy – this should take about 5 minutes. Gradually beat in the eggs, until combined.

3 Alternately beat the flour mixture and the soured cream into the butter bowl until completely combined. Beat in the vinegar, bicarbonate of soda and food colouring. Spoon the mixture into the prepared tin and level the surface.

4 Bake for 1 hour–1 hour 10 minutes until a skewer inserted into the centre comes out clean. Cool in the tin for 10 minutes, then turn out on to a wire rack (leave the lining paper on) and leave to cool completely. When the cake is cold, peel off the lining paper, then halve the cake horizontally.

5 To make the frosting, put the cream cheese and butter into a large bowl and beat together until combined.

Cuts into 10 slices

Sift in the icing sugar and mix well. Spread about half the icing over the bottom half of the cake, then sandwich back together. Spread the remaining icing over the top of the cake and decorate with sugar sprinkles, if you like.

SAVE TIME

Store in the fridge. It will keep for up to two days. Allow to reach room temperature before serving.

Chocolate Roulade

Hands-on time: 25 minutes
Cooking time: about 15 minutes, plus cooling

150g (5oz) plain chocolate (at least 70%
   cocoa solids), broken into pieces

5 large eggs, separated

150g (5oz) caster sugar

1 tbsp cornflour

cocoa powder to dust

For the topping

125ml (4fl oz) double cream

75g (3oz) plain chocolate, finely chopped

2 tbsp golden syrup

silver and gold balls, plus edible glitter,
   to decorate

For the filling

150ml (¼ pint) double cream

1 tbsp icing sugar

1 Preheat the oven to 180°C (160°C fan oven) mark 4. Line a shallow 33 × 23cm (13 × 9in) baking tin with baking parchment. Melt the chocolate in a heatproof bowl over a pan of gently simmering water, making sure the base of the bowl doesn't touch the water. Leave to cool.

2 Put the egg yolks and caster sugar into a large bowl and, using a hand-held electric whisk, beat until pale and thick – this should take about 5 minutes. Fold in the cooled chocolate. In a separate bowl and using clean beaters, whisk the egg whites and cornflour until they form soft peaks. Using a large metal spoon, fold the whites into the chocolate mixture – be careful not to knock out too much air. Spoon the mixture into the prepared tin and tilt the tin to spread the mixture evenly.

3 Bake for 12–15 minutes, then take out of the oven and cover with a damp teatowel. Leave to cool.

4 Meanwhile, make the topping. Put the cream into a pan and bring just to the boil, then take off the heat and stir in the finely chopped chocolate until melted. Stir in the golden syrup and leave to cool.

5 To make the filling, lightly whip the cream and icing sugar in a bowl until the cream just holds a shape.

6 Put a sheet of greaseproof paper a little larger than the baking tin on a damp teatowel. Lightly dust the paper with cocoa powder. Invert the cake on to the paper, then remove the tin and peel off the lining paper. Spread the cream filling over the cooled cake. Using the greaseproof paper to help, roll up the cake from one of the short ends. Make the first turn as tight as possible so that the cake will roll up evenly and have a good shape when finished. Once rolled, put seam-side down on a platter. Spread the topping over the roulade, then using a fork, mark with ridges to resemble bark. Decorate with silver and gold balls and edible glitter. Serve in slices.

Chocolate Roulade (see previous page)

Cuts into 8 slices

Chocolate Wedding Cake (see overleaf)

Serves 40

Chocolate Wedding Cake

Hands-on time: 1 hour 25 minutes, plus chilling
Cooking time: about 2 hours, plus cooling

350g (12oz) butter, chopped, plus extra
   to grease
350g (12oz) plain chocolate, chopped
275ml (9fl oz) milk
375g (13oz) plain flour
3 tsp baking powder
65g (2½oz) cocoa powder
750g (1lb 11oz) caster sugar
6 medium eggs
250ml (9fl oz) soured cream

For the decoration
350g (12oz) plain chocolate, chopped
mixed berries (such as raspberries,
   strawberries, blackberries and
   blueberries)
icing sugar to dust

For the filling
175g (6oz) white chocolate, chopped
250g (9oz) unsalted butter, softened
500g (1lb 2oz) icing sugar
3 tbsp milk

1 Preheat the oven to 160°C (140°C fan oven) mark 3. Grease a 25.5cm (10in) round cake tin and line with baking parchment.

2 Put the butter, chocolate and milk into a pan and heat gently until smooth and glossy. Leave to cool slightly.

3 Sift the flour, baking and cocoa powders into a large bowl, then stir in the sugar. In a separate large jug, mix together the eggs and soured cream. Pour both the chocolate and egg mixtures into the flour bowl and whisk until combined. Pour the mixture into the prepared tin and level the surface.

4 Bake in the centre of the oven for about 2 hours or until a skewer inserted into the centre comes out clean. Cool completely in the tin.

5 Meanwhile, make the chocolate and fruit decoration. Cover two large baking sheets or trays with baking parchment and secure in place with some tape.

6 Melt the plain chocolate in a heatproof bowl over a pan of gently simmering water, making sure the base of the bowl doesn't touch the water. When smooth, take off the heat and pour half on to each sheet. Spread the chocolate so that it is just shorter in length than the baking sheet and twice the height of the cake plus 7.5cm (3in) in width. Chill for 10 minutes.

7 Using a large, non-serrated knife, trim the edges of the chilled chocolate to neaten, then cut in half lengthways. Now cut across rectangles in parallel lines, about 4cm (1½in) apart. If you like, trim one end of each small rectangle at an angle, then chill again until solid.

8 To make the white chocolate filling, melt the chocolate in a heatproof bowl over a pan of gently simmering water, making sure the base of the bowl doesn't touch the water. When melted and smooth, lift the bowl off the pan and leave to cool for 15 minutes.

9 Put the softened butter into a separate large bowl and sift the icing sugar over. Using a hand-held electric whisk and starting slowly, beat together until fluffy and combined. Beat in the cooled chocolate and the milk.

10 When ready to decorate, turn the cooled cake out of the tin and peel off the lining paper. If necessary, use a bread knife to level the top of the cake. Slice the cake in half horizontally.

11 Spread about half the buttercream over the bottom half of the cake, then sandwich the two halves together. Next, smear a little buttercream on a cake board the same size as the cake and stick the cake on to the board. Spread the remaining buttercream sparingly over the cake. Working quickly before the buttercream sets, stick chocolate shards to the side of the cake. Arrange the berries to cover the surface of the cake and dust lightly with icing sugar.

Classic Christmas Cake

🍴 **Hands-on time:** 1 hour, plus three days' soaking and 24 hours' drying
Cooking time: about 4 hours, plus cooling

500g (1lb 2oz) sultanas

400g (14oz) raisins

150g (5oz) each Agen prunes and dried figs, roughly chopped

200g (7oz) dried apricots, roughly chopped

grated zest and juice of 2 oranges

200ml (7fl oz) hazelnut liqueur, such as Frangelico Hazelnut Liqueur, plus extra to drizzle

250g (9oz) unsalted butter, softened, plus extra to grease

150g (5oz) each dark muscovado and light soft brown sugar

200g (7oz) plain flour, sifted

1 tsp ground cinnamon

1 tsp mixed spice

¼ tsp ground cloves

¼ tsp freshly grated nutmeg

a pinch of salt

4 large eggs, beaten

100g (3½oz) toasted blanched hazelnuts, roughly chopped

40g (1½oz) toasted pinenuts

1 tbsp hazelnut liqueur or brandy (optional)

For the icing

4 tbsp apricot jam

icing sugar, sifted, to dust

450g pack ready-to-roll marzipan

vegetable oil to grease

500g pack royal icing sugar

For the decoration

150g (5oz) glacier mint sweets

75cm (30in) silver ribbon, 2cm (¾in) wide

silver candles

1 Put the fruit into a non-metallic bowl and stir in the orange zest and juice and the hazelnut liqueur. Cover and leave to soak overnight or, preferably, up to three days.

2 Preheat the oven to 140°C (120°C fan oven) mark 1. Grease a 23cm (9in) cake tin and double-line with greaseproof paper, making sure the paper comes at least 5cm (2in) above the top of the tin. Grease the paper lightly, Then wrap a double layer of greaseproof paper around the outside of the tin and secure with string – this will stop the cake burning.

3 Put the butter and sugars into a large bowl and, using a hand-held electric whisk, beat together until light and fluffy – this should take about 5 minutes.

4 In a separate bowl, sift together the flour, spices and salt. Beat 2 tbsp of the flour mixture into the butter and sugar, then gradually add the eggs, making sure the mixture doesn't curdle. If it looks as if it might be about to, add a little more flour.

5 Using a large metal spoon, fold the remaining flour into the mixture, followed by the soaked fruit and the nuts. Tip into the prepared tin and level the surface. Using the end of the spoon, make a hole in the centre of the mixture, going right down to the bottom of the tin – this will stop the top of the cake rising into a dome shape as it cooks.

6 Bake for 4 hours or until a skewer inserted into the centre comes out clean (if necessary, cover the top of the cake loosely with foil if it appears to be browning too quickly). Leave to cool in the tin for 10 minutes, then turn out on to a wire rack, keeping the greaseproof paper wrapped around the outside of the cake, and leave to cool completely.

7 To store, leave the cold cake in its greaseproof paper. Wrap a few layers of clingfilm around it, then cover with foil. Store in a cool place in an airtight container. After two weeks, unwrap the cake, prick all over and pour 1 tbsp of hazelnut liqueur over it, or brandy if you like. Rewrap and store as before. Ice up to three days before serving.

8 When ready to ice the cake, gently heat the jam in a pan with 1 tbsp water until softened, then press through a sieve into a bowl to make a smooth glaze. Put the cake on a board and brush the top and sides with the glaze.

9 Dust a rolling pin and the worksurface with a little icing sugar and roll out the marzipan to a round about 15cm (6in) larger than the cake. Position on the cake and ease to fit around the sides, pressing out any creases. Trim off the excess around the base. Leave to dry for 24 hours.

10 To make the mint shard decoration, preheat the oven to 180°C (160°C fan oven) mark 4. Line a baking sheet with foil and brush lightly with oil. Unwrap the mints and put pairs of sweets on the baking sheet about 1cm (½in) apart, leaving 5cm (2in) of space between each pair, to allow room for them to spread as they melt. Cook for 3–4 minutes until the sweets have melted and are just starting to bubble around the edges. Leave to cool on the foil for 3–4 minutes until firm enough to be lifted off. Use kitchen scissors to snip the pieces into large slivers and shards.

11 Wrap the ribbon around the bottom edge of the cake. Put the icing sugar in a bowl and make up according to the pack instructions. Using a small palette knife, spread the icing over the top of the cake, flicking it into small peaks as you go. Then tease the edges of the icing down the sides of the cake to form 'icicles'.

12 While the icing is still soft, push the mint shards into the top of the cake and insert the silver candles. Leave the cake to dry. Light the candles and serve in slices.

SAVE TIME

Complete the recipe up to the end of step 7 (before icing), wrap and store for up to three months. It can be doused in alcohol every week if you like a stronger taste.

Cuts into 24 slices

321 cal ♥ 4g protein 17g fat (10g sat) ♥ 0.5g fibre ♥ 42g carb ♥ 0.2g salt

12

520 cal ♥ 6g protein 30g fat (19g sat) ♥ 1g fibre 62g carb ♥ 0.4g salt

14

with cream - 241-321 cal 4-6g protein ♥ 9-12g fat (5-6g sat) ♥ 0.4-0.5g fibre 39-51g carb ♥ 0.1g-0.1g salt

16

302 cal ♥ 6g protein 17g fat (10g sat) ♥ 0.3g fibre 34g carb ♥ 0.2g salt

20

555 cal ♥ 7g protein 31g fat (11g sat) ♥ 2g fibre 63g carb ♥ 0.5g salt

34

350 cal ♥ 6g protein 18g fat (8g sat) ♥ 2g fibre 45g carb ♥ 0.4g salt

36

200 cal ♥ 4g protein 3g fat (0.7g sat) ♥ 0.5g fibre ♥ 41g carb ♥ 0.9g salt

38

for 8: 424 cal ♥ 6g protein 25g fat (13g sat) ♥ 1g fibre 46g carb ♥ 0.3g salt

56

185 cal ♥ 3g protein 1g fat (trace sat) ♥ 2g fibre 42g carb ♥ 0.1g salt

58

393 cal ♥ 4g protein ♥ 23g fat (14g sat) ♥ 0.8g fibre 47g carb ♥ 0.7g salt

60

359 cal ♥ 6g protein 17g fat (2g sat) ♥ 1g fibre 49g carb ♥ 0.5g salt

72

140 cal ♥ 3g protein 5g fat (3g sat) ♥ 0.9g fibre 22g carb ♥ 0.7g salt

74

60 cal ♥ 2g protein 1g fat (trace sat) ♥ 0.5g fibre ♥ 12g carb ♥ 0.2g salt

76

386 cal ♥ 3g protein 17g fat (11g sat) ♥ 1g fibre 58g carb ♥ 0.5g salt

80

Calorie Gallery

303 cal ♥ 6g protein
22g fat (13g sat) ♥ 1g fibre
22g carb ♥ 0.2g salt

12

579 cal ♥ 7g protein
40g fat (22g sat) ♥ 2g fibre
52g carb ♥ 1g salt

26

for 10: 363 cal ♥ 3g protein
18g fat (11g sat) ♥ 1g fibre
50g carb ♥ 0.4g salt

28

582 cal ♥ 9g protein
46g fat (23g sat) ♥ 1g fibre
35g carb ♥ 0.3g salt

30

497 cal ♥ 7g protein
19g fat (10g sat) ♥ 2g fibre
80g carb ♥ 0.4g salt

32

without marzipan carrots:
697 cal ♥ 7g protein
48g fat (18g sat) ♥ 1g fibre
62g carb ♥ 0.9g salt

46

569 cal ♥ 6g protein
29g fat (17g sat) ♥ 0.8g fibre
78g carb ♥ 0.8g salt

48

436 cal ♥ 6g protein
28g fat (13g sat) ♥ 2g fibre
44g carb ♥ 0.5g salt

50

384 cal ♥ 5g protein
20g fat (10g sat) ♥ 2g fibre
48g carb ♥ 0.5g salt

32

325 cal ♥ 6g protein
21g fat (11g sat) ♥ 1g fibre
30g carb ♥ 0.3g salt

66

405 cal ♥ 7g protein
24g fat (14g sat) ♥ 2g fibre
44g carb ♥ 0.8g salt

68

220 cal ♥ 4g protein
7g fat (3g sat) ♥ 0.5g fibre
37g carb ♥ 0.1g salt

70

256 cal ♥ 4g protein
8g fat (1g sat) ♥ 0.8g fibre
45g carb ♥ 0.2g salt

32

291 cal ♥ 5g protein
13g fat (6g sat) ♥ 2g fibre
42g carb ♥ 0.1g salt

84

303 cal ♥ 5g protein
18g fat (7g sat) ♥ 1g fibre
33g carb ♥ 0.3g salt

88

387 cal ♥ 4g protein
21g fat ♥ (13g sat) ♥ 0.5g fibre
47g carb ♥ 0.2g salt

90

374 cal ♥ 4g protein
18g fat (11g sat) ♥ 0.7g fibre
52g carb ♥ 0.4g salt

94

563 cal ♥ 8g protein
34g fat (11g sat) ♥ 1g fibre
60g carb ♥ 0.3g salt

96

480 cal ♥ 4g protein
25g fat (15g sat) ♥ 0.9g
fibre 65g carb ♥ 0.6g salt

98

405 cal ♥ 5g protein ♥ 21g
fat (11g sat) ♥ 0.9g fibre
53g carb ♥ 0.4g salt

100

230 cal ♥ 4g protein
6g fat (1g sat) ♥ 1g fibre
42g carb ♥ 0.1g salt

112

333 cal ♥ 4g protein
22g fat (11g sat) ♥ 1g fibre
31g carb ♥ 0.5g salt

114

218 cal ♥ 5g protein
2g fat (trace sat) ♥ 2g fibre
49g carb ♥ 0.5g salt

116

228 cals, 4g protein
7g fat (4g sat) ♥ 1g fibre
40g carb ♥ 0.5g salt

118

210–243 cal ♥ 2–3g protein
12–14g fat (8–9g sat)
1–1g fibre ♥ 27–30g carb
0.1–0.1g salt

128

515 cal ♥ 6g protein
31g fat (15g sat) ♥ 2g fibre
59g carb ♥ 0.4g salt

136

440 cal ♥ 5g protein
22g fat (12g sat) ♥ 1g fibre
59g carb ♥ 0.8g salt

140

567 cal ♥ 5g protein
49g fat (22g sat) ♥ 2g fibre
54g carb ♥ 0.3g salt

146

425 cal ♥ 3g protein
8g fat (3g sat) ♥ 0.4g fibre
86g carb ♥ 0.2g salt

156

724 cals ♥ 7g protein
53g fat (33g sat) ♥ 1g fibre
58g carb ♥ 1.4g salt

158

480 cal ♥ 7g protein
31g fat (18g sat) ♥ 1g fibre
45g carb ♥ 0.1g salt

160

410 cal ♥ 4g protein
21g fat (13g sat) ♥ 1g fibre
55g carb ♥ 0.2g salt

164

282 cal ♥ 3g protein
13g fat (8g sat) ♥ 0.4g fibre
41g carb ♥ 0.3g salt
02

385 cal ♥ 4g protein
26g fat (16g sat) ♥ 1g fibre
♥ 36g carb ♥ 0.5g salt
104

542 cal ♥ 8g protein
33g fat (13g sat) ♥ 2g fibre
56g carb ♥ 0.6g salt
106

171 cal ♥ 2g protein
7g fat (4g sat) ♥ 0.4g fibre
28g carb ♥ 0.3g salt
108

368 cal ♥ 6g protein
19g fat (11g sat) ♥ 1g fibre
47g carb ♥ 0.8g salt
20

233 cal ♥ 4g protein
8g fat (5g sat) ♥ 0.8g fibre
38g carb ♥ 0.4g salt
122

137 cal ♥ 4g protein
1g fat (trace sat) ♥ 2g fibre
31g carb ♥ 0.3g salt
124

236 cal ♥ 4g protein
9g fat (4g sat) ♥ 1g fibre
37g carb ♥ 0.5g salt
126

590 cal ♥ 5g protein
42g fat (25g sat) ♥ 1g fibre
50g carb ♥ 0.7g salt
48

546 cal ♥ 7g protein
23g fat (11g sat) ♥ 2g fibre
83g carb ♥ 0.6g salt
150

456 cal ♥ 8g protein
29g fat (13g sat) ♥ 1g fibre
40g carb ♥ 0.5g salt
152

659 cal ♥ 7g protein
45g fat (25g sat) ♥ 1g fibre
60g carb ♥ 0.3g salt
154

(un-iced) 375 cal ♥ 5g protein 14g fat (6g
sat) ♥ 3g fibre 56g carb ♥ 0.1g salt
(iced) 569 cal ♥ 6g protein ♥ 17g fat (6g sat)
3g fibre ♥ 100g carb ♥ 0.2g salt
66

Index

PICTURE CREDITS

Photographers: Steve Baxter (page 91); Martin Brigdale (page 15); Nicki Dowey (pages 43, 59, 69, 113, 115, 117, 119, 123, 125, 137, 147 and 157); Emma Lee (page 141); William Lingwood (pages 21, 27, 64B, 109, 142, 143 and 162); Gareth Morgans (pages 29, 335, 47, 49, 63, 73 and 151); Myles New (pages 153 and 163); Craig Robertson (pages 11, 52, 53, 54, 55, 64T, 75, 127 and 144); Lucinda Symons (pages 17, 23, 3, 37, 39, 67, 71, 77, 81, 83, 85, 89, 95, 97, 99, 101, 103, 105, 107, 121 and 129); Martin Thompson (pages 13 and 169); Phillip Webb (pages 51, 149 and 155); Kate Whitaker (pages 57, 61 and 159).

Home Economists:
Joanna Farrow, Emma Jane Frost, Teresa Goldfinch, Alice Hart, Lucy McKelvie, Kim Morphew, Aya Nishimura, Bridget Sargeson and Mari Mererid Williams.

Stylists: Tamzin Ferdinando, Wei Tang, Helen Trent and Fanny Ward.

BAKE ME A CAKE
There's always time for cake

EASY PEASY MEALS
Easy meals for every day

LET'S DO BRUNCH
Mouth-watering meals to start your day

CHEAP EATS
Budget-busting ideas that won't break the bank

SALAD DAYS
Oh-so-fresh ideas for fabulous salads

Available online at store.anovabooks.com and from all good bookshops

POSH NOSH
Delicious recipes to impress your guests

PARTY FOOD
Delicious recipes to get the party started

SLOW STOPPERS
Slow-cooked meals packed with flavour

GREAT VEG
Inspired ideas for delicious veggie meals

AL FRESCO EATS
Easy grills, barbecues and picnics

ROAST IT
There's nothing better than a delicious roast

FLASH IN THE PAN
Spice up your noodles and stir-fries

GLUTEN-FREE AND EASY
Oh-so-good-for-you recipes that taste great

LOW FAT LOW CAL
Nice recipes don't need to be naughty